TONY STEWART

HIGH OCTANE
IN THE FAST LANE

TONY STEWART

HIGH OCTANE
IN THE FAST LANE

Sports Publishing L.L.C.
Publisher: **Peter L. Bannon**
Senior Managing Editors: **Joseph J. Bannon, Jr. and Susan M. Moyer**
Art Director: **K. Jeffrey Higgerson**

Graphic Designer: **Christine Mohrbacher**
Coordinating Editor: **Lynnette Bogard**
Copy Editor: **Cynthia L. McNew**

Front cover photo:
Steve Helber, AP/Wide World Photos
Back cover photo:
Craig Jones, Getty Images

ISBN: 1-58261-260-9

SP
**SPORTS
PUBLISHING
L.L.C.**

Table of Contents

Rookie Stewart Claims First Career Winston Cup Victory 7

Stewart Wins Race; Jarrett Avoids Disaster 13

Jarrett Wraps Up Championship; Stewart Wins Again 17

Top Rookie Sets Tough Standard for Future 23

Stewart Sweeps at Dover 27

Stewart Wins from Pole at Martinsville 33

Stewart Close to Another Record 37

Stewart Wins Competitive Race at Daytona 43

Gordon and Stewart at it Again 53

Memory of Big Daytona Crash Doesn't Deter Stewart 57

Stewart Wins Pontiac 400 at Richmond 63

Stewart Hopes New Diet Helps in Doubleheader 67

Stewart Fresh After 1,100 Miles on the Track 71

Stewart Takes Dodge-Save Mart 350 on the Road Course 77

Stewart Ignores Black Flag, Subject to Stiff NASCAR Penalty 81

Stewart Feels Emptiness on Return to Loudon 87

Stewart Forgives and Forgets His Way to Victory 91

Stewart Makes Noise, Hears Plenty 95

Stewart Uneasy About Head-and-Neck Restraints 101

Stewart Puts Turbulent 2001 Behind Him 105

Defending Champion Stewart Cherishes Shootout Victory 109

Stewart Holds Off Earnhardt for Atlanta Victory 115

A Patient Stewart Rules Again at Richmond 119

No Double Duty for Stewart 127

Stewart Still Hears Boos, But Not As Many 131

Defending Champ Stewart Earns Pole at Sears Point 135

Brickyard 400: Pressure Builds As Indiana's Stewart Wins Pole 143

Driver Stewart Wins at Watkins Glen 149

"I had won a bunch of races in my life, and deep down, I believed I could win at the Winston Cup level. But believing and knowing are two different things. The higher up you get in this sport, the truer that gets."

—Tony Stewart on his first Winston Cup victory

ROOKIE STEWART CLAIMS FIRST CAREER WINSTON CUP VICTORY

By HANK KURZ Jr., AP Sports Writer

October 12, 1999

RICHMOND, Va. (AP)—Tony Stewart's performance through his first 24 races on the Winston Cup circuit made it clear to almost everyone that he wasn't just an average rookie content to take his licks and learn as much as he could.

Too often Stewart contended in races only to have a late mistake or some misfortune cost him a chance at victory. But he kept coming back strong, and it seems everyone expected Stewart to visit Victory Lane sooner rather than later.

But when it finally happened on Saturday night, with Stewart turning the usually exciting Exide 400 into a race that merely validated what so many others already knew, the 1997 IRL champion seemed humbled, even surprised.

"It's unbelievable. I would have never dreamed that I would have gotten here, first of all, let alone gotten the opportunity to win," he said. "To do it in my rookie season, I think it's going to hit even harder tomorrow morning."

Hampered early by slower pit stops than the rest of the leaders, Stewart made up for it with that rare car that was the fastest on both short and long runs.

He led 333 laps in all, including the last 144, and said it was even sweeter that the only car in striking distance at the end was that of Bobby Labonte, his teammate for owner Joe Gibbs and one of his mentors in his first season.

"The neatest thing about the whole race was the last lap," Stewart said. "I got to the middle of the backstretch and I hear 'Hey Tony.' It was Bobby. He had changed the frequency on his radio to mine. I was in the middle of [Turns] three and four and he said, 'Good job.' I hadn't even won the race yet.

"I think he may have been trying to trick me and he wanted me to lift a little early and he could drive on by," Stewart joked. "That just shows the support that this team has. I couldn't be more fortunate to have a teammate like Bobby."

Labonte, who finished 1.114 seconds behind in the battle of Pontiacs, was thrilled for Stewart.

"That's huge," he said. "When I won at Charlotte in '95, that was the biggest night of my life. It just boosts your confidence that much more. It's great."

The night also proved special for Gibbs, who surprised his rookie driver with a congratulatory message in Victory Lane as Stewart made his victory lap.

"It was one of the big thrills of my life," Gibbs said over the track's PA system. "I'm so happy for Tony. He's raced his guts out all year."

Stewart said he'd been thinking about Gibbs at the end, too.

"I was thinking to myself after we took the checkered [flag], 'If he's not here, I don't think I'm going to let him come to any more races this year.'"

Stewart became only the sixth Winston Cup rookie to win in his first year and only the second driver to gain his first career victory on the three-quarter-mile Richmond International Raceway oval. Kyle Petty was the first, 13 years ago.

Points leader Dale Jarrett bounced back from two off weeks that cut his 314-point lead almost in half by finishing third, boosting his lead over Mark Martin back to 270 points. Martin had engine trouble with 35 laps left and finished 35th.

"It's nice to gain some points again," Jarrett said. "It shows what kind of race team this is. They bounced back from the last two weeks and they bounced back from the first half of a race that wasn't that great and continued to battle."

Jeff Gordon, who ran in the top five for the first 305 laps, lost his clutch right after losing the race out of the pits and went to the garage shortly thereafter. He failed to finish for the sixth time this season and wound up 40th.

Sterling Marlin was fourth, followed by Kenny Irwin and Dale Earnhardt.

"When you're a good young race driver, like Tony is, you just want to do everything."

—Parnelli Jones

STEWART WINS RACE; JARRETT AVOIDS DISASTER

By MIKE HARRIS, AP Motorsports Writer

 November 7, 1999

AVONDALE, Ariz. (AP)—Tony Stewart came of age Sunday, dominating the Checker Auto Parts-Dura Lube 500K, a race in which Dale Jarrett barely avoided disaster and took another step toward his first Winston Cup championship.

Stewart won for the second time this season, matching the rookie record set in 1987 by the late Davey Allison.

"I never would have thought we could have won one race," said Stewart, who previously won in Richmond, Va., on Sept. 11. "We knew the team was capable, but I didn't think they had a driver who knew how to win this year."

"They won that race for us in the pits... When you have Mark Martin in your mirrors, chasing you hard, you need all the edge you can get."

—Tony Stewart

The 28-year-old Stewart started 11th in the 43-car field and took control of the race on the 159th of 312 laps around the one-mile Phoenix International Raceway oval.

The only time Stewart trailed the rest of the way was during a green-flag pit stop sequence. But even the stops worked in his favor as his Joe Gibbs Racing crew got him in and out in a hurry.

"They won that race for us in the pits," he said. "On the last stop [on Lap 268], we went from a second and a half ahead to three seconds ahead. When you have Mark Martin in your mirrors, chasing you hard, you need all the edge you can get. That three-second lead made me feel a lot more comfortable."

Stewart's Pontiac beat Martin's Ford to the finish line by 2.081 seconds, a lead of nearly a full straightaway.

Jarrett, who came into the race leading Bobby Labone by 246 points in the championship chase, looked like a real contender early the race, although pole winner John Andretti led the first 43 laps.

Jarrett led 50 of the first 148 laps. Then came trouble for the 42-year-old son of two-time series champion Ned Jarrett.

The first of only two caution flags in the race waved on Lap 121 when Brett Bodine cut down a tire and tagged

TONY STEWART

the wall. On the ensuing restart, Jarrett was right behind Martin when the latter couldn't get up to speed immediately because of a failed ignition.

Jarrett slammed into the rear of Martin's car at the head of a long line of traffic, but they were both able to get up to speed after a brief hesitation.

"It's a good thing that was Dale Jarrett behind me," Martin said. "I was able to switch to the other ignition box and took off."

Jarrett grabbed the lead back on Lap 129, two laps after the restart, but the incident eventually caused a near disaster for the No. 88 team.

On Lap 149, Jarrett began to lose ground. The next lap, he slowed on the backstretch, his right front tire going flat, apparently from the contact with Martin.

He pitted for right side tires and his Robert Yates Racing crew got Jarrett back onto the track a lap down, but just barely behind leaders Andretti and Stewart.

Jarrett, now 26th, went after the leaders, passing Stewart on Lap 158 and then drove past Andretti on Lap 159 as Stewart followed him by to take the lead.

After that Jarrett just kept moving through the pack. After the last caution of the day, brought out by Sterling Marlin's blown engine on Lap 182, assured Jarrett of staying on the lap, he was able to move back among the leaders.

He finished sixth, just behind next season's teammate Ricky Rudd, and will head into next Sunday's inaugural Winston Cup race in Homestead, Fla. leading Labonte by 231 points.

"It was just one of those things that I've been talking about," Jarrett said. "I was sitting there leading the race and the car's in great shape and we have a flat tire.

"You lose a lap and then it's a struggle from there. But the guys did a fantastic job in the pits gaining us some positions."

Jarrett can wrap up the $2 million title simply by finishing eighth or better next week, or by finishing ninth and getting the five-point bonus for leading at least one lap. Even if he has a bad day in Homestead, all Jarrett has to do to win is finish 30th or better in each of the last two races to close out Labonte.

"Bobby gained a few points on us, but not too many," Jarrett said. "We go to Homestead next week and do our job, and if we finish in the top 10, that should pretty much do it for us."

Labonte, who finished third, just ahead of Jeff Burton and Andretti, said, "I have no idea what the [points] lead is. If we go to Miami and run good, it'll take care of itself."

"What first caught my attention was that Tony was a versatile driver, and very few of them come along. I kind of admired him."

—A. J. Foyt

JARRETT WRAPS UP CHAMPIONSHIP; STEWART WINS AGAIN

By MIKE HARRIS, AP Motorsports Writer

 November 13, 1999

HOMESTEAD, Fla. (AP)—New champion Dale Jarrett may have taught rookie Tony Stewart a lesson Sunday, even though it was Stewart who won the inaugural Pennzoil 400.

Jarrett, knowing he had only to finish eighth or better to clinch his first Winston Cup title, drove to a solid fifth-place finish at Homestead-Miami Speedway.

"He did exactly what he had to do and he did it with class," the 28-year-old Stewart said of Jarrett, who will turn 43 on Nov. 26. "He's a great person. You can learn a lot from somebody like that.

"He's been consistent, and that's what wins championships. He deserves it."

Stewart stood in the spotlight following his second straight win, something no other rookie has done in NASCAR's 52-year history. But he shared it easily with Jarrett.

"Fantastic!" Jarrett yelled after emerging from his No. 88 Ford. "I've just got to thank God for the talent on this race team and putting me here with such great people."

He stayed in the top 10 throughout the 267-lap race and goes into the season finale next week in Atlanta 211 points ahead of runner-up Bobby Labonte, with a maximum of 185 remaining.

Jarrett's consistent performance this season—four victories, 23 top fives and 28 top 10s in 33 starts—gave Robert Yates his first title since he became a car owner in 1989.

Jarrett led the championship race from the 11th race, May 11 in Richmond, Va.

"We were running well, we were consistent and we weren't having any problems," he said. "That's when I knew we were kind of in control of our own destiny and if we didn't mess up and do crazy things that this could happen."

Jarrett admitted it was hard for him to keep his emotions in check as the season stretched on and the championship came within reach. When the checkered flag waved, it was not elation he felt at first.

"There was a little relief that we had done it, it was over with," Jarrett said. "I think the feeling of accomplishment hit me more than anything."

After he got out of the car and celebrated with his team, the excitement grew.

"I apologize to Bobby Labonte. I made a rookie mistake and drove into him. I just went in there too hard and couldn't hold my line. But I was trying to win the race."

—Tony Stewart

"It's just incredible," he said. "It's better than I ever thought it was going to be."

Jarrett and his father, Ned, who won two series championships, join Lee and Richard Petty as the only father-son combinations to win NASCAR titles.

The younger Jarrett, who was considered simply a journeyman early in his career, blossomed into a star when he moved into the No. 88 car in 1996. He had finished third, second and third in the last three years.

Stewart and Labonte, teammates at Joe Gibbs Racing,

exchanged the lead several times in the late going. Labonte had dominated most of the way, leading four times for 174 laps.

Stewart, who led four times for 43 laps, is the first NASCAR driver to win three races in his rookie season, breaking the mark of two set by the late Davey Allison in 1987.

The 28-year-old driver took the lead from Labonte on a pit stop on Lap 187 during the only caution of the 400-mile race, which resulted from Ricky Rudd's blown engine.

Labonte wouldn't let his teammate get away, passing him for the lead on Lap 200 in the battle of Pontiacs. But Stewart regained the top spot with a pass on Lap 229.

The race then came down to the last pit stops, with Labonte making his stop for a splash of gas and two tires on Lap 244 and Stewart doing the same four laps later.

As Stewart raced off pit lane and back onto the 1.5-mile oval near the exit of Turn 2, he came out alongside Labonte. The two ran side by side for a few agonizing moments. Then Stewart's car slid up the track and bumped his teammate, who slipped behind.

"I apologize to Bobby Labonte," Stewart said. "I made a rookie mistake and drove into him. I just went in there too hard and couldn't hold my line. But I was trying to win the race."

Labonte, who saw any possible hopes of catching Jarrett in the points disappear with that pass, accepted the apology.

"I don't think it mattered," he said. "I wouldn't have beat him anyway. I couldn't figure out my tires today. That was my fault."

Stewart moved in front for the final time on Lap 258. He took the lead when Mark Martin made his final stop and easily pulled away. He won by 5.289 seconds, nearly a full straightaway.

With only five laps under caution, Stewart's average speed was 140.335. He won $278,265.

His third victory of the season breaks the mark set in 1987 by the late Davey Allison, and his 12 top five finishes is also a rookie best, topping the 11 by Dale Earnhardt in 1979.

The victory also solidified Stewart's hold on fourth place in the points—a finish which would be the best by a first-year driver in NASCAR's modern era—dating to 1972.

Jeff Burton finished third on Sunday, followed by Martin, Jarrett, Mike Skinner and Kyle Petty, the only other drivers on the lead lap at the end.

"I don't care what level of racing we're talking about. The name of the game is winning."

—Tony Stewart

TOP ROOKIE SETS TOUGH STANDARD FOR FUTURE

By MIKE HARRIS, AP Motorsports Writer

November 24, 1999

Tony Stewart's rookie performance in the Winston Cup series certainly got the attention of Dale Earnhardt Jr.

"That was the best rookie year ever," said the two-time Busch series champion, who moves up next year with sidekick Matt Kenseth to NASCAR's premier races. "How the heck do Matt and me follow something like that?"

It won't be easy.

Stewart had a rookie-record three victories and a fourth-place finish in the standings—the best by a first-timer in the 29 years of the series. He raised the bar of excellence much higher.

To approach it, the best freshman of 2000 will need to bond with his crew chief the way Stewart did with fellow novice Greg Zipadelli.

"I don't know why we had such great chemistry," Stewart said. "It's either there or it's not. It was there right away with Greg Zipadelli. It was there from our first test session."

Even with good chemistry, it took a while to reach high gear. Stewart began with finishes of 28th, 12th, 36th and 11th before a pair of sixth-place runs offered a hint of what was to come.

"At the beginning of the season, I was a little nervous and tentative about what I was doing in the car," said Stewart, the 1997 Indy Racing League champion. "All it took was getting in lots of laps and a lot of miles."

He got them with a lot of testing early in the season. And he cherishes the advice from Joe Gibbs Racing teammate Bobby Labonte, who wound up second to Dale Jarrett in the standings.

"My confidence level from the beginning of the year to now is just quadrupled many times over," the 28-year-old Stewart said. "I'm so confident in these cars now."

Zipadelli conceded halfway through the season that inexperience hurt the team early on. They should have won more races, he said after a painful defeat in July,

when Stewart dominated in New Hampshire only to lose because of an ill-advised gamble on fuel.

But no one scored more points in the second half of the season.

Stewart's 32-year-old crew chief looks at those numbers as a reason for optimism next season. And he isn't alone. Many in the sport are predicting a championship for Stewart.

"We're pretty excited about next year," Zipadelli said. "We just feel like we've got a little something to look back at now."

What they will see are more numbers that reflect a great season. Stewart was running at the end in all but one of the 34 races. He had 12 top five finishes and 21 top 10s.

In any other year, it could be argued that Earnhardt or Kenseth would have a chance to be the greatest rookie ever. But in 2000, they've got quite an act to follow.

"I hope nobody expects us to match what Tony did," Kenseth said. "He was amazing.

"I'll be pretty happy if I reach my goals, and they won't be anywhere near what he did."

Even Earnhardt's father, the only driver to go from Rookie of the Year to series champion, and three-time champion Jeff Gordon didn't come close to matching Stewart's first-year numbers.

Like Stewart, Gordon came into stock car racing with an open-wheel background. Unlike Stewart, he struggled at first and wound up 14th in the standings as the top rookie of 1993.

He marvels at Stewart's progress.

"He's made the transition to these cars faster than anybody else has," Gordon said. "That's a special gift.

"There's no doubt that Tony is the real thing."

Gibbs, who as coach of the Washington Redskins won three Super Bowls before becoming a car owner in 1992, is not easily impressed. He expected great things from Labonte but said earlier in the season that a top 20 finish in points would have been acceptable from Stewart.

"It's hard to believe what all of the people on this team accomplished this year," Gibbs said. "I think everybody knew Bobby was headed in that direction and was going to be a big star in this sport, but maybe Tony surprised some people with what he did."

The only way he can surprise anybody next season is by failing to have a great one.

"Just being satisfied has never been enough for me. That's not what got me here."

—Tony Stewart

STEWART SWEEPS AT DOVER

By DICK BRINSTER, AP Sports Writer

September 24, 2000

DOVER, Del. (AP)—Tony Stewart isn't thinking much about anything but how to run the next lap or win the next race.

His numbers in two seasons of Winston Cup racing are gaudy by any standards, but he'll let everybody else decide what they mean.

"If anybody had told me I'd have seven wins by this time in my second year, I would have told them they were crazy," Stewart said Sunday after winning the MBNA.com 400 at Dover Downs International Speedway.

The victory was his fourth this year, tying Rusty Wallace for the series lead. In 1999, Stewart set records for success by a rookie. Now, he has a chance to lead the circuit in wins, something Jeff Gordon has done five years in a row.

But Stewart doesn't worry about that or his prospects for winning the championship in 2001.

"We want to go on winning every week, but it's not like we're in a competition to see who can win the most races," he said. "We just want to win as many as we can."

If anything, Stewart is a bit disappointed he's 459 points behind teammate Bobby Labonte in the standings. After finishing a rookie-record fourth in points last year, Stewart is fifth.

He is driven by the need to constantly improve, and some bad finishes have hurt him.

"We just want to get back our consistency," he said. "Even if we have to trade this win today for five top fives, I would do it because consistency is worth more than wins."

He's right about that, and his 4-3 edge in victories counts far less than Labonte's 13-8 advantage in top five finishes.

Stewart concedes that he thinks about future championships and even considered winning one as a rookie. But he says two seasons on the circuit have demonstrated just how difficult that is to accomplish.

"I'm seeing what Bobby is doing this year and realize how to do it," Stewart said. "I've won more races than he has, but I'm so far behind him in points I could never catch him.

"I don't want to be a guy who wins tonight and then comes back to finish 32nd next week."

On Sunday, Stewart became the first driver to sweep the races at Dover Downs International Speedway since Jeff Gordon in 1996.

He did so after a bad beginning to the weekend. He started 27th in a field of 43. In June, when he won the MBNA Platinum 400, the driver from Rushville, Ind., started 16th.

Stewart downplayed the importance of starting first.

"Poles are nice, but you get to take the picture with the big trophy on Sunday," he said. "We know we run good on Sunday, and we're putting an emphasis on winning races."

Crew chief Greg Zipadelli is confident that they will continue to do just that in the coming years.

"When he gets on rhythm, I don't think anybody is better out there," Zipadelli said.

Still, he was talking to his driver on the radio Sunday, urging him forward but with a sense of caution. Later, Stewart laughed at that.

"I think he was trying to calm himself down," he said of his crew chief. "I said, 'If I go any slower, the car's going to fire me.'"

Stewart ended a run of three straight wins in this race by Mark Martin, who had a transmission problem and wound up sixth. He was one of several drivers to have problems.

Stewart led 163 of the 400 laps, including the last 54. In June, he led 242.

The win ended an eight-race losing streak for the 1999 Winston Cup Rookie of the Year.

Jeff Burton, who led every lap a week earlier while winning in Loudon, N.H., and Jerry Nadeau were among those who had the look of winners. But they fell out with blown tires. At least five cars left the race that way.

"How can you beat Goodyear?" asked Tony Furr, Nadeau's crew chief. "If I brought a car to the race track that was that bad, I'd be fired. It was just a junky tire."

Zipadelli admitted the race made him somewhat uneasy, but said he was never concerned about Stewart having a problem.

"We seem to be very conservative in that area at most race tracks," Zipadelli said. "We'll finish second or fifth before we take a chance on ruining a race car or hurting a driver."

Labonte's lead in the series standings grew to a season-high 249 points with a fourth-place finish. Burton and reigning Winston Cup champion Dale Jarrett, who crashed early in the race, were the biggest losers.

Their troubles allowed seven-time champion Dale Earnhardt to move into second place with a finish of 17th. Jarrett finished 32nd to remain third, 267 points back. Burton wound up 36th and fell to fourth in the title race, a point behind Jarrett

"Tony was just a little too tough, which is OK," said Johnny Benson, who matched a career best with a finish of second. "We'll take second and get out of here."

Ricky Rudd, a four-time winner at Dover, finished third.

"I think everybody felt all along like Tony had real talent and that he would run up front at some point in Winston Cup. But I don't think anybody guessed that he'd have done what he's done this quickly. He amazes me."

—Joe Gibbs, team owner

STEWART WINS FROM POLE AT MARTINSVILLE

By HANK KURZ Jr., AP Sports Writer

October 1, 2000

MARTINSVILLE, Va. (AP)—The way Tony Stewart has been dominating at Martinsville Speedway, he's bound to eventually learn to like the place.

Stewart kept the lead through the final set of pit stops and quickly ended runner-up Dale Earnhardt's chances of making it a duel by pulling away over the final 11 laps Sunday for his second consecutive victory.

"We're getting closer," Stewart said of the track, where he started on the pole twice this season, each time setting a qualifying record. "I feel like I've made great gains here, and I feel like [crew chief Greg Zipadelli] and the guys have made great gains here as well.

"You can't do it by yourself."

Stewart pulled away from The Intimidator to win the NAPA 500 by .672 seconds. It was his Winston Cup-leading fifth victory this year, the eighth of his career and the third time he's won back-to-back races.

Doing it this time with the black car of one of racing's fiercest competitors in the rear view mirror of Stewart's Pontiac made it better.

"He didn't get the nickname The Intimidator for nothing," Stewart said of Earnhardt, a seven-time series champion. "He's as tough as they come ... I knew it was going to be the toughest 11 laps of my life probably."

Instead, it was much easier than the roaring crowd anticipated.

"I couldn't catch him," said a disappointed Earnhardt. "If I could have got to him, it would have been good, but I couldn't catch him."

Earnhardt outlasted Jeff Burton for second and gained 36 points on championship leader Bobby Labonte with six races left on the schedule.

"It's going to take a whole lot of gaining and a whole lot of him finishing back there," Earnhardt said of Labonte, who now leads by 213 points. "I know we didn't gain a whole lot on him today, but we gained."

Ricky Rudd finished fourth, followed by Jeff Gordon and Dale Jarrett.

Stewart, who has said all week that Martinsville isn't his favorite track, said he was spurred on by booing that lasted throughout the race.

"I want to thank those three guys at the back of the grandstand," he said. "They kept booing us all day and that pumped me up more than anything."

The race seemed to be shaping up as a classic short track event, and when the 13th and final caution flew on the 481st lap, the crowd roared because it erased Stewart's large lead and gave Earnhardt a chance.

But the green flag on Lap 490 was a go for Stewart to win.

Labonte, who overcame a lot of bad luck to finish 10th, was happy.

"It was a good day," he said. "To come out of Martinsville 10th with everything that happened today—it could have been a lot worse."

Burton passed series champion Dale Jarrett for third, 227 points back, but left the track 60 miles from his South Boston home dejected.

"We had a great car. We had great pit stops," he said, blaming crowding on pit lane for his being beaten out of the pits at the end. "You don't have a lot of chances to win these things."

Burton appeared to have the strongest car for much of the race and led 202 of the first 467 laps. But Dave Blaney's spin brought out the 12th caution, ending 101 laps of green-flag racing, and jumbled things up.

Sterling Marlin took only two tires and was first out of the pits, followed by Stewart, Gordon, Burton and Earnhardt. Stewart need only two laps to pass Marlin, Earnhardt close behind, and it never changed.

"It was a good race, and it came down to a good race at the end," Earnhardt said. "And that's what it's all about in short track racing."

"I want to thank those three guys at the back of the grandstand. They kept booing us all day and that pumped me up more than anything."

—Tony Stewart

Labonte's recovery from repeated bad luck ended up being one of the biggest stories of the day, keeping him on pace for the championship.

With about 215 laps to go, all the leaders pitted under caution.

Labonte, who went onto pit road in fifth place, was on his way out when Earnhardt cut off Rudd, causing a backup that ended with Labonte getting pinched by two other cars, damaging the front of his Pontiac.

Labonte pitted twice more under the yellow to have the damage fixed, then was running 26th when it went back to green with 209 laps left.

After working his way back into the top 10, Labonte was bumped by Mike Skinner coming out of the fourth turn with 23 laps remaining.

The bump caused Labonte's car to spin in a cloud of smoke with cars passing on both sides. But he regained control and sped off, having lost just one position on the track.

"Tony has been very impressive. I've really enjoyed his performance and it was absolutely that: a special performance."

—Bobby Allison

STEWART CLOSE TO ANOTHER RECORD

By DICK BRINSTER, AP Sports Writer

November 1, 2000

Tony Stewart wasn't content with his record-setting rookie season. So he went out this year as a sophomore and did it again, taking one checkered flag after another.

With a victory Sunday at Phoenix International Raceway, he will turn the best rookie season in Winston Cup history into the most productive ever by a second-year driver.

Nonetheless, Stewart isn't concerned about his place in history.

"I don't think we're even looking at that," he said. "We want to go out and win every week, but it's not that we're in a competition to see who can win the most races."

A victory would be his sixth this season, one more than Dale Earnhardt had when he set the record for second-year drivers in 1980. It also would guarantee Stewart no worse than a tie for the most wins this year, which no sophomore driver has ever done.

"Winning is great," he said. "But this is all about consistency and points and championships. I'd rather have five top fives than a win."

With three races remaining, only Rusty Wallace and Bobby Labonte—with four victories apiece—loom as reasonable threats to win more than Stewart. But his position appears solid because the race Sunday and the one a week later in Homestead, Fla., are on tracks where Stewart won last year.

So for the first time since 1994, someone other than Jeff Gordon—who remains a distant contender with three victories—should lead the circuit. Could it be the start of a roll for the 29-year-old Stewart?

"We just want to go out and get the best we can out of our car in every race," said Stewart, who also would have to lead the next four years to match Gordon's series record of five in a row. "I'm not thinking about that. This is all about focusing on the next race."

Crew chief Greg Zipadelli doesn't see many problems with the team, but he also doesn't know if that means a championship is in its future.

"Last year, we said we had to grow in some areas," he said. "This year, we'll look back on the season and say we have to grow in some other areas in order to be a championship contender."

In 1999, when Stewart set rookie records with three victories and a final standing of fourth in the points, he was running at the end of all but one of the 34 races.

> "I'd love to have one of those killer seasons that only happen from time to time at the Winston Cup level. I'm talking about a year when you leave no doubt that you were the baddest team in town, whether you win the championship or not."
>
> —Tony Stewart

He got behind in points because of accidents and mechanical problems early this season and is sixth in the series despite leading in victories.

"Our consistency is what has hurt us this year," Zipadelli said. "We haven't had many boring days. We're always battling back from something."

The team's ability to overcome problems is what impresses Zipadelli the most. He says Stewart often has come from a lap or more down in his two seasons to finish in the top five.

Zipadelli knows leading the circuit in victories is great, but he is driven in part by the ones that got away.

"We probably had chances at five or seven other races that we weren't able to capitalize on," he said.

Joe Gibbs Racing is at the top with Stewart and teammate Labonte, who's closing in on his first series title. Stewart says Gibbs, whose Washington Redskins won three Super Bowls, is a great motivator, especially in the down times.

"We'll have a bad race and Greg will be throwing things in his office and I'm destroying my house," Stewart said. "Joe can get us calmed down and look ahead rather than back to a bad day."

But Gibbs's easygoing demeanor isn't a given, Stewart insists. He knows what some of the Redskins might have heard during a few of the coach's tirades.

"I've only seen him mad about three times, but he was justified every time," Stewart said. "When he does get mad he gets everybody's attention in a hurry. It just doesn't happen that often."

41

"Any win at Daytona is an accomplishment to cherish, but to beat Earnhardt there was an amazing feeling."

—Tony Stewart

STEWART WINS COMPETITIVE RACE AT DAYTONA

By MIKE HARRIS, AP Motorsports Writer

February 10, 2001

DAYTONA BEACH, Fla. (AP)—Daytona needed a competitive race and got it in Sunday's Budweiser Shootout.

Tony Stewart outdueled Dale Earnhardt at the head of a 14-car pack to win the made-for-TV race for last year's NASCAR pole winners.

More important, with complaints about last year's sleeper of a Daytona 500 still remembered, the stock car sanctioning body's new aerodynamic package turned the 70-lap, 175-mile event into an exciting show for the 75,000 spectators.

45

"I think it made it better," Stewart said of the aero changes that included a metal strip across the top of the car and an extension on the rear wing. The new package slows the cars by up to 10 mph and adds considerable drag.

"It put a little more of the driving and our fate back into our hands," Stewart said. "Guys had to let up and even brake at times."

Earnhardt took the top spot from Stewart as the two drove into the third turn on the 2.5-mile oval with two laps remaining. But Stewart's Pontiac was too strong, sweeping past Earnhardt's famed No. 3 Chevrolet on the next lap—the last of 19 lead changes among seven drivers.

Stewart, whose Joe Gibbs Racing teammate Bobby Labonte won the Winston Cup championship last season, showed he is likely to be a force in 2001. He led four times for a race-high 36 laps and pulled away to beat seven-time champ Earnhardt by 0.145 seconds— about two car lengths.

The green flag stayed out for the entire race, and 16 of the 18 starters—including three former Shootout winners and one wild card selection from second-round qualifying leaders—were running at the end.

Stewart, who earned $202,722 from the $900,000 purse, averaged 181.036 mph.

The race, which was extended this year from a 25-lap sprint and is now considered a true preview of the 500-mile race, might have been decided on the 25th lap anyway when a handful of drivers, including Earnhardt, made their one scheduled pit stop. Stewart and most of the other competitors waited until Lap 45 for their stops.

"I wanted to wait to the last lap to make my move on him, but it was the first move I got on him all day," Earnhardt said. "With this aero package, you've got to take it when you can get it.

"His car was strong and his tires were fresher," the 1998 Daytona 500 winner added. "I don't know if that [early stop] was the right call or not. If I could have stayed side by side with him, I could have raced him. But I just couldn't do that."

Asked about the handling of the cars, Earnhardt said, "I think you saw a better race. NASCAR works hard to keep everybody even and they've done a good job."

Mike Helton, NASCAR's president, was beaming following the race.

"I thought it was a good show," Helton said.

Fords driven by Rusty Wallace, defending Daytona 500 winner Dale Jarrett and Jeff Burton finished third through fifth, followed by Dale Earnhardt Jr. and Labonte.

Other drivers in the lead pack at the end were Mark Martin, Ricky Rudd, Mike Skinner, Jeff Gordon, Bill Elliott, Joe Nemechek and Steve Park.

Wallace never was able to get a run at the two leaders and finished just behind Earnhardt.

"I learned a lot today about how to maneuver around with these new rules, and I learned a lot from watching Dale today," Wallace said. "It was a little nerve-racking the way the cars were handling, but it's a little too early to make a judgment."

Elliott, who won the pole for next Sunday's featured race in qualifying Saturday, never got into contention with the only one of the new Dodge Intrepids in the race.

"We learned quite a bit," the two-time Daytona winner said. "The biggest thing we needed to do was run the whole race. We're encouraged. We just need to work on our handling package a little."

Stewart, whose Joe Gibbs Racing
teammate Bobby Labonte won the
Winston Cup championship last season,
showed he is likely to be a
force in 2001.

"I absolutely believe that I'm hungrier than the next guy is."

—Tony Stewart

GORDON AND STEWART AT IT AGAIN

By JENNA FRYER, AP Sports Writer

March 26, 2001

BRISTOL, Tenn. (AP)—At the height of their feud last season, Jeff Gordon threatened to knock Tony Stewart into a wall the next chance he had.

It took him six months, but he finally got a measure of revenge when he sent Stewart into a spin in the final turn at Bristol Motor Speedway.

The tap sent Stewart up the high banking toward the outside wall. Stewart's retaliation—he raced around the track on the cool-down lap and hit Gordon on pit road—rekindled the rivalry between two of NASCAR's biggest names.

On Monday, NASCAR fined Stewart $10,000 and placed him on probation until Aug. 29.

Both drivers played down the bumps, the first of which cost Stewart a top five finish.

"I've got no hard feelings against Jeff, and I don't think he has any against me," Stewart said.

That's not how it looked Sunday, when the two resumed a feud that dates back at least to last August.

Gordon had been chasing Stewart for fourth place

for several laps when they entered Turn 3 on the last lap Sunday. Gordon slid down to pass Stewart, but the cars touched.

Stewart spun out; Gordon slid past him and finished fourth. Stewart ended up 25th after straightening his car out and motoring across the finish line.

Although it initially appeared that Stewart struck the wall, his car only shot up Bristol's 36-degree banking and stalled after spinning.

He then hustled around the track on the cool-down lap in pursuit of Gordon, who had entered pit row by the time Stewart caught him.

Stewart made a hard left into the pits, maneuvered through the traffic and rammed into the back of Gordon. The hit caused Gordon to spin out and slam the retaining wall, and an in-car camera showed Stewart giving Gordon an obscene gesture as he drove off.

"That didn't surprise me a bit," Gordon said of the retaliation.

Gordon and Stewart have been battling since last August, when the two clashed at Watkins Glen, N.Y., when Stewart sent Gordon into a wall.

They ended up in a shouting match when Stewart went to Gordon's hauler to apologize, and Gordon promised Stewart he would knock him into a wall "the next chance I get."

All eyes were on them the next week, when the two again tangled on the track. Once again, Stewart knocked Gordon out of the race, but afterward they both chalked the incident up as a racing accident.

The feud soon simmered down, but the rivalry between the two former open-wheel racers has obviously lingered—proven Sunday.

"We're both open-wheel racers who are stock car racers now, and we're both aggressive and we both want to win and we both want to get every spot we can every time we're on the race track," Stewart said. "We just had a meeting of the minds in the last quarter of the last lap of a 500-lap race."

The latest incident earned them both a meeting with NASCAR officials after the race. Before Gordon spoke with officials, he defended his actions and said Stewart should have seen him attempting to pass him.

"I thought it was pretty clean," Gordon said. "I did everything I could do to keep from hitting him. I didn't want it to come down to the last lap like that, but if you've got a position and you've been working on it a long time, you're going to do it and you're going to take everything you can all the way to the end."

Gordon had no comment after his brief meeting with NASCAR.

Stewart's time before the sanctioning body lasted much longer than Gordon's.

"It's just racing," he said.

Last week, NASCAR fined Busch Series drivers Ryan Newman and Tim Fedewa $5,000 each and placed them both on probation for the rest of the season for hitting each other after the race.

Stewart's penalty might have harsher because he hit Gordon on pit road, when crew members and NASCAR officials were not protected and could have been injured had Gordon's car spun another way.

Stewart apologized for that.

"I spun him on the pit lane and that was wrong," Stewart said. "I could have hurt somebody, in all reality."

"Most times when I'm racing, I'm too busy to be scared."

—Tony Stewart

MEMORY OF BIG DAYTONA CRASH DOESN'T DETER STEWART

By MIKE HARRIS, AP Motorsports Writer

April 19, 2001

Tony Stewart worried? Nah.

Despite the wild 19-car crash in the season-opening Daytona 500, Stewart isn't concerned about a possible repeat Sunday at Talladega.

"It's just another race to me," Stewart said. "As far as my accident is concerned ... it was a racing accident. It's over with and I'm fine."

Stewart went airborne and landed on Bobby Labonte's roof before barrel-rolling to a stop midway down the backstretch at Daytona International Speedway.

"If anything, walking away from a crash like that gives me more confidence to get back into the car knowing it's as safe as any engineer has ever seen for a Winston Cup car,"

—Tony Stewart

Stewart, the top Winston Cup rookie in 1999 and last year's leading race winner with six, doesn't worry because he knows his Joe Gibbs Racing Pontiac is safe.

"If anything, walking away from a crash like that gives me more confidence to get back into the car knowing it's as safe as any engineer has ever seen for a Winston Cup car," he said.

"We had engineers who specialize in analyzing those types of crashes come to the race shop after Daytona to look at our car, and they said it was the best car they had seen preparation-wise as far as safety was concerned."

Dale Earnhardt was killed on the final turn of the Daytona race in a crash that looked far less dangerous than the earlier one. The death of his friend and competitor bothers Stewart far more than the possibility of being involved in another wreck.

"There's still a part of it that's going to be hard to deal with at Talladega," Stewart said. "But I think that he'd want us to go on and do the best that we all can, and that's what we'll do."

> "It's just another race to me. As far as my accident is concerned ... it was a racing accident. It's over with and I'm fine."
>
> —Tony Stewart

TONY STEWART

"I am doing the only thing I ever really wanted to do and the only thing that completely fulfills me. I'm a very lucky person."

—Tony Stewart

"Tony's going to be one kick-ass racer; at some point, he's going to have a period, three or four years in a row, where he'll be one of the most dominant guys."

—Dale Earnhardt Jr.

STEWART WINS PONTIAC 400 AT RICHMOND

By HANK KURZ Jr., AP Sports Writer

May 5, 2001

RICHMOND, Va. (AP)—With a one-second lead and seven laps remaining, the only flags Tony Stewart hoped to see were a white one and then a checkered one.

He got more than that, starting with a yellow, then a red. But neither was enough for Jeff Gordon, Rusty Wallace or other contenders to prevent Stewart from winning the Pontiac Excitement 400 Saturday night.

"This is probably the most competitive Richmond race I've ever been a part of," said Stewart, who got his first Winston Cup victory here in 1999. "So many cars and so many drivers were so fast all night long that on any

given run, there were five or six guys that had potential to lead."

It was Stewart, however, who won every duel. He was prepared to win another one with only a few laps to go, too.

Thanks to Wallace and Gordon, it never happened, allowing Stewart to pull away on a restart with two laps remaining and win with ease.

"I thought NASCAR was going to take it away from me," Stewart said of the final restart, which came after Dave Blaney hit the wall with seven laps to go and NASCAR red-flagged the race to set up a stirring finish.

"The last two laps the car slid around all over the place," Stewart said. "I had my hands full. My car skated around to the checker."

The battle turned out to be between Gordon, who was running second, and his rival Wallace, who was third, but got a great jump on the leaders.

Pulling even inside Gordon heading into Turns 1 and 2, Wallace ended up running Gordon up the track, both cars avoiding contact. But that removed them from contention as Stewart went on to win by .372 seconds.

"I just got too loose there at the very end," Wallace quipped about the bumping duel with Gordon. "Not much I could do about that."

Gordon was livid when he confronted Wallace after the battle; both drivers were animated as they exchanged what appeared to be harsh words.

"He body-slammed me pretty good and I got pretty mad at him," Gordon said after collecting himself. "There was no reason for him to slam me. I mean it was just racing, but I was a little mad at him, you know?"

Stewart, much to his delight, would have had a great view of the whole thing—in his rearview mirror—if he had had time to watch it unfold.

Stewart had a lead of more than a second until Blaney hit the wall in Turns 3 and 4 with seven laps to go, bringing out the eighth caution.

The crowd roared its approval when NASCAR then red-flagged the event with five to go so safety crews could make sure the track was clean and safe. NASCAR then used two caution laps to prepare for the final sprint.

That left two laps of green-flag racing, and when the green flew, so did Stewart, Gordon and Wallace. But when Wallace pulled even with Gordon and ran him up the banking in Turn 2, it gave Stewart clear sailing.

Gordon finished second, followed by Wallace, and the two rivals bumped several times on the cool-down lap, in the same spot where Wallace ran Gordon into the wall several years ago, costing him a possible victory.

The red flag proved very costly for points leader Dale Jarrett, whose car ran out of gas during the delay and had to be pushed around the track to his pits. Jarrett dropped from eighth to a 15th-place finish.

Jarrett's lead in the standings fell from 66 to 14 over Gordon, with Wallace climbing past Johnny Benson into third, 62 points back.

Stewart, who had a series-high six victories last year

but had not won since October in Martinsville, won for the 10th time in his career.

He earned it more than once.

Running third with 70 laps to go, Stewart caught up to Ricky Rudd and spent 20 laps ducking under and around him, trying to get by. He finally did on the backstretch with 50 to go, then went looking for Wallace.

Wallace, the career leader with six victories on the three-quarter-mile Richmond International Raceway, had led five times for 276 laps, but his lead was shrinking and it seemed just a matter of time for Stewart.

Passing Wallace must have seemed like a replay of his battle with Rudd for Stewart, but he quickly pulled even, they traded the lead a few times and Stewart took it for good on the 362nd lap, quickly pulling away.

Steve Park rallied late for fourth, followed by Rudd, Benson and defending race champion Dale Earnhardt Jr.

> *"My relationship with my team is stronger than ever. The most important thing is that I've got really solid bonds with the people I need to work most closely with as a driver."*
>
> —Tony Stewart

STEWART HOPES NEW DIET HELPS IN DOUBLEHEADER

By JENNA FRYER, AP Sports Writer

May 23, 2001

CONCORD, N.C. (AP)—Tony Stewart hasn't eaten a doughnut in weeks and he can barely remember the taste of pizza.

He has traded his cheeseburgers and chili fries for broiled chicken and steamed broccoli.

It hasn't been easy. For most of his 30 years, the NASCAR star has been addicted to fast food.

"I have nothing against people who eat a lot of health food and like to stay healthy, but I like my pizzas and burgers," Stewart said.

So why change?

In a span of 12 hours Sunday, he plans to race in the Indianapolis 500 and Coca-Cola 600. Two years ago, Stewart failed to prepare his body for 1,100 miles of competition.

Consumed with avoiding dehydration, Stewart ate only some mini-bagels and a health food bar on race day.

"I drank so much, I swore I was a fish—I thought I could breathe under water," he said. "But I didn't eat any solid foods with enough nutrients in it.

"How did I know? I'm not a nutritionist, I'm a race car driver."

The oversight was costly. After finishing ninth—four laps down—at Indy, Stewart flew to Charlotte and wound up fourth in the Coca-Cola 600.

Exhausted at the end of the race, after completing 1,090 of a possible 1,100 miles on the day, Stewart had to be helped from the car and taken on a stretcher to the care center at Lowe's Motor Speedway.

He vowed never to attempt the feat again but was lured back to Indy when the team that won last year offered him a ride. Along for the whole trip will be Al Shuford, the trainer for Joe Gibbs Racing, which fields Winston Cup cars for Stewart and Bobby Labonte.

Shuford says suppressing Stewart's urge for fast food is easier than it was two years ago.

"I tell people that he has been like a butterfly coming out of a cocoon," Shuford said. "Even if it was chewing leaves and jumping up and down out of a tree. If I told him to go do that he would probably do that, because that's how dedicated and how focused he is."

Only once in the past few weeks has Stewart strayed, and it came with Shuford's blessing. Running late to catch a plane last week, Stewart stopped at a drive-thru for a quick bite.

But no burgers and fries. Shuford limited Stewart to a fish sandwich.

"It was a little reward, not too big, but something to make him feel good about how hard he's been working," Shuford said.

Stewart will be more careful about what he eats on race day, and he plans to have a bowl of pasta on the trip from Indianapolis to Charlotte.

To understand Stewart's commitment to this venture, one needs only to hear him talk about his childhood in Indiana.

Growing up 45 minutes from Indianapolis Motor Speedway, Stewart raced home from school every day in May to turn on the television and find out how things were going at the track. Like a lot of young Hoosiers, he just had to race in the 500.

In 1996, he realized his boyhood dream and even won the pole. He finished 24th, leaving with an engine failure.

Stewart was fifth in 1997, when he won the Indy Racing League championship. In 1998, he finished last, leaving after just 22 laps with another engine problem.

The next year, his record-breaking rookie season in Winston Cup, Stewart became only the second driver

to complete the Indy-Charlotte double. Although he has admitted fatigue hurt him in the Coca-Cola 600, Stewart's Winston Cup team understands his decision to return to Indy.

It would have been hard for Stewart to say no when Chip Ganassi offered him the ride in which Juan Montoya won the race last year. Stewart will start seventh Sunday.

"Everyone has dreams and goals that they set for themselves, and Tony made it clear before he ever signed the first contract with us that this is something that he wanted to do," said J. D. Gibbs, president of Joe Gibbs Racing. "We thought about it and kind of gave him a list of things. We thought if he could meet these objectives then it wouldn't be a problem, and he has met them all."

One of those requirements is getting to the Coca-Cola 600 on time. With such tight time constraints, Stewart might be forced to abandon the 500 during the race.

"They're pretty generous in letting me do this," Stewart said. "Saying that at a certain time I have to be out of the IRL car to make sure that I start this race on time, I don't think that is unreasonable."

After his exile from the drive-thru line, Stewart should consider it just another sacrifice.

"I like my life. I'm having the kind of career that once would have been just a crazy dream."

—Tony Stewart

STEWART FRESH AFTER 1,100 MILES ON THE TRACK

By DAVID DROSCHAK, AP Sports Writer

13

May 28, 2001

CONCORD, N.C. (AP)—Tony Stewart wasn't looking for a bed or a juicy T-bone steak after his 1,100 miles of racing.

To the contrary.

"Are there any dirt tracks where we can race at tonight?" Stewart asked after finishing off a long day on a pair of superspeedways with a third-place finish at the Coca-Cola 600. "If there was, I'll tell you what, I'd go right now."

Seven hours earlier Sunday, the race-aholic came in sixth at the Indianapolis 500 before jetting to North Carolina for his second stab at the grueling racing double.

> ## "Are there any dirt tracks where we can race at tonight?" If there was, I'll tell you what, I'd go right now."
>
> —Tony Stewart

"I'm pretty pumped up," said Stewart, who almost caught second-place finisher Kevin Harvick after starting last in the 43-car field instead of 12th because he missed the mandatory driver's meeting. "The doctor asked me how I felt after the race and I said, 'Heck, we were the fastest race car on the track the last 30 laps.'"

In 1999, Stewart had to be pulled from his stock car at Lowe's Motor Speedway and placed on a stretcher after finishing fourth as he nearly collapsed when he failed to eat properly during his first attempt at the racing double.

This time around, Stewart was better prepared with a doctor and trainer helping him stay fit and on a proper diet.

"I wish I would have eaten what I normally would have eaten two years ago to see what would have happened," said Stewart, who finished ninth at Indy in '99. "I made a big mistake by worrying too much about what I was drinking and not worrying at all about what I was eating."

Stewart, 30, said the hardest part of this racing double wasn't any pass or tricky track surface, but getting stuck with a needle while getting fluids on his plane ride to North Carolina.

"I thought I was going to pass out," he said.

While Stewart was happy about his performance, he was on edge when asked about reporters who raised questions about safety issues of racing so many miles in one day.

He called them idiots and said he was hurt by fan reaction.

High Octane in the Fast Lane

"I read a couple of letters fans wrote about how selfish I was and I was putting the other drivers at risk and I wasn't taking care of Joe Gibbs Racing," Stewart said. "It took a lot away from what I was going to do. I didn't feel good about going back to Indianapolis [Saturday night].

"But to do what we did, I think it was worth it. I don't think any of those other drivers felt like I put them at risk."

Coca-Cola 600 winner Jeff Burton said he didn't have a problem with Stewart's attempt to win both races in one day.

"I have no issue with it at all," Burton said. "Where did he finish tonight? Third. That's a helluva good day. I'm proud of him for doing it.

"A couple of years ago he wasn't fit enough to do it. If he couldn't have gotten it done, he would have pulled it in."

Less than five minutes after finishing at Indy, Stewart was whisked to a helicopter behind the infield care center. The next stop on his racing odyssey was an airplane bound for North Carolina, where he landed 50 minutes before the start of the longest NASCAR Winston Cup race.

He arrived at Lowe's at 5:07 p.m.—18 minutes ahead of schedule. He even made it in time for driver introductions, where he was booed.

Stewart looked fresh as he waved to the fans when he exited the helicopter wearing his Home Depot racing uniform, passing on a golf cart ride as he walked to the podium at the start-finish line.

But Stewart made an early mistake in his second race of the day, spinning out in the second lap as he tried to weave his way through the field, bringing out the race's first caution flag.

He radioed to crew chief Greg Zipadelli that he was too impatient with his early move.

Stewart's car suffered some damage to the right front when he hit the rear of Kurt Busch's Ford, and he pitted four times during the race's first 14 laps—all under caution.

It didn't take Stewart long to rebound, moving up to 12th by the midway point in the race and sixth after 252 laps.

And few argued he had the best car at the end.

"If he would have stayed here all day in his [qualifying] spot he probably would have won," Harvick said.

Stewart disagreed, saying his stock car was way too loose early in the race to be running in heavy traffic.

"As far off as we were at the beginning of the race, at least we were out of everybody's way for the most part," Stewart said.

Stewart refused to say if he'll attempt double duty again. He wanted time to savor a pair of top 10 finishes.

"I wouldn't change the way we've done anything the last three weeks, that's for sure," Stewart said. "I got out of the car on my own, I walked to the trailer on my own, changed clothes on my own. For somebody that ran the full 1,100 miles, I feel pretty good."

"When they wave that green flag, I guarantee you I'm going to drive with as much heart as anybody in the field."

—Tony Stewart

STEWART TAKES DODGE-SAVE MART 350 ON THE ROAD COURSE

By ANNE M. PETERSON, AP Sports Writer

June 24, 2001

SONOMA, Calif. (AP)—Even though Tony Stewart wasn't sure he had the Dodge-Save Mart 350 in the bag, he offered his crew some encouraging words with a few laps to go.

"I said, 'We're gonna win this thing,'" Stewart said.

He went on to grab his second win of the year and his 11th career victory under partly cloudy skies on the hilly road course at Sears Point Raceway.

In the process, he spoiled Robby Gordon's bid for a first victory and Jeff Gordon's push for a Winston Cup record.

With 11 laps to go, leader Robby Gordon was fighting off brushes by charging rookie points leader Kevin Harvick—who was trying to get back on the lead lap—and missed Stewart's deft pass on Turn 7 to take the top spot.

"I'm not sure I did anything better," Stewart said. "I was just in the right place at the right time."

Robby Gordon, who started in seventh, was subbing for Ultra Motorsports driver Mike Wallace in a Ford. He finished second, 1.746 seconds behind Stewart.

"Kevin knocked me sideways and I honestly didn't anticipate Tony to get by both of us," Robby Gordon said. "I thought he would be on the inside."

Pole-sitter Jeff Gordon was vying for his record-setting seventh road course victory as well as his fourth straight win at Sears Point. He finished third after leading 32 of the 112 laps in his Chevy and remains the Winston Cup points leader.

"All good streaks have to come to an end eventually," Jeff Gordon shrugged.

Stewart, whose Pontiac started the race third, also won this year in Richmond, Va. His first road course victory came in just his fifth start on a serpentine layout.

"I never ran a road race in anything other than go-karts," he marveled.

The former Rookie of the Year banged on the top of his car as he got out, then embraced his crew.

"This was a big win for us today—especially being able to beat Jeff Gordon," he said.

Sears Point, one of two road courses on the Winston Cup series, is currently undergoing a $35 million renovation. It was reduced this year to 10 turns for NASCAR events but lengthened to two miles.

Jeff Gordon, the three-time series champion, has four poles this season along with three victories. He leads the circuit with 11 top five finishes.

"We got a solid finish, and that's all I was asking for," he said. "I know you guys had me winning the race before it started, but I didn't expect that ... I think Tony had the best car there at the end."

Ricky Rudd drove his Ford to a fourth-place finish, followed by Rusty Wallace, who started his Ford alongside Gordon in the front row.

Wallace, Gordon, Richard Petty and Bobby Allison have six road course victories apiece.

Ron Fellows, a road course specialist driving for NEMCO Motorsports, led for 20 laps after a caution on the 32nd lap. It was the first time he had led a Winston Cup race since August 1999 in Watkins Glen, N.Y., where the circuit races in August.

There were five cautions for 17 laps in the race, which featured eight different leaders.

Harvick finished 14th in his Chevy. He was unhappy afterward about Robby Gordon's efforts to hold him off.

"You're leading the race; what do you do?" he asked. "You let the guy behind you go. He's a lap down and it doesn't mean anything to you. You protect your spot from the guy in second."

Robby Gordon was unapologetic.

"I think when you're a race car driver and you can put a lapped car between you and second place, you do it," he said.

"I can live with getting outrun, but getting robbed—by a competitor or an official, it doesn't matter—is something else altogether. And maybe I don't always handle that in the most graceful way, but damn it, this is my career, my life."

—Tony Stewart

STEWART IGNORES BLACK FLAG, SUBJECT TO STIFF NASCAR PENALTY

By JENNA FRYER, AP Sports Writer

July 7, 2001

DAYTONA BEACH, Fla. (AP)—Tony Stewart was severely punished by NASCAR on Saturday night for breaking a strict racing rule and ignoring a black flag in the final laps of the Pepsi 400.

Stewart, who drew the black flag for driving below the yellow line on the race track, was docked 20 finishing positions—a punishment that cost him 65 points in the standings.

Long before the punishment was announced, an angry Stewart tried to argue his case with NASCAR officials.

But he was rebuffed in his effort to approach Winston

"He's a fierce competitor and to us, we didn't think it was fair,"

—Greg Zipadelli, Crew Chief

Cup director Gary Nelson at the NASCAR hauler and had to be restrained by car owner Joe Gibbs and his crew chief.

Stewart also slapped a reporter's tape recorder away and kicked it under a hauler.

Gibbs then went into the NASCAR hauler to speak to Nelson as the on-track incident was reviewed.

Stewart, already on probation until August for hitting Jeff Gordon's car on pit road earlier this season, left the track without commenting long before NASCAR announced its penalty.

"He's a fierce competitor and to us, we didn't think it was fair," crew chief Greg Zipadelli said. "We were looking at it one way and we don't think it's fair. We just went in to debate our side, but a decision is a decision."

NASCAR spokesman John Griffin said Stewart would face further penalties for his postrace behavior.

Stewart was running in second place with four laps to go as he neared the start/finish line. With a pack of cars behind his Pontiac challenging him for position, he slid his car down on the track below the yellow line on the bottom of the track.

That's a strict rules violation in NASCAR that the drivers were reminded of during their prerace meeting.

"This is your warning," events director David Hoots said at the meeting. "If you go below the line, you will be penalized. I don't want to see you in the trailer complaining about it afterward, because you have been warned."

So when Stewart's left-side tires went below the line, Hoots immediately called him into the pits for the black flag.

But Stewart, who was one of five drivers eligible for a $1 million bonus if he won the race, ignored the order. His defense for breaking the rule was that he was forced below the line when Johnny Benson, Jeremy Mayfield and Bobby Labonte all tried to pass him in a four-wide pack.

Zipadelli said Stewart absolutely believes Benson forced him below the line and NASCAR should have considered that.

"I think there are some circumstances at times that put people in that situation," he said. "It's a very sensitive situation and we were one of those people. You've got to treat people with respect. It's three laps to go and we're racing for a million dollars.

> "We made a judgment call. He was shown the black flag and he disobeyed it. He was warned about going under the yellow line in the drivers' meeting and told that it would not be tolerated, and it wasn't."
>
> —Danielle Humphrey, NASCAR spokeswomen

"But we have to live and go on with the decision that they made."

The shuffle pushed Stewart back to seventh place and he ultimately finished sixth.

But after a 90-minute review of the situation, in which NASCAR officials watched a video of the infraction from several angles, the sanctioning body ruled against him.

As punishment, his official finishing order was moved from sixth to 26th, making him the last car to finish on the lead lap.

"We made a judgment call," NASCAR spokeswoman Danielle Humphrey said. "He was shown the black flag and he disobeyed it. He was warned about going under the yellow line in the drivers' meeting and told that it would not be tolerated, and it wasn't."

Humphrey was not sure if Stewart would face further penalties.

But the initial ruling was costly enough—he lost 65 points in the standings, a critical blow in his bid to win his first Winston Cup championship.

Stewart entered the race fourth in the points standings, 89 behind leader Gordon. By taking away his finishing order, he retained his spot in the standings but fell 201 points back.

"It's costly for us," Zipadelli said. "With the points being as important as they are and really honestly feeling like we still had a shot at the championship. It could have been a huge night for us and it turns out to be maybe one of the most disappointing nights in my career."

"Through nine years of rivalry, there's been a mutual admiration and respect for one another and for what each other could do in a race car. I've said this a thousand times since I started in Winston Cup: Kenny's part of the reason I got here, because he pushed me to make myself better each week."

—Tony Stewart

Tony Stewart leaves Memorial Services for Kenny Irwin.

STEWART FEELS EMPTINESS ON RETURN TO LOUDON

By EDDIE PELLS, AP Sports Writer

July 19, 2001

LOUDON, N.H. (AP)—For almost a decade, Tony Stewart and Kenny Irwin were more rivals than friends, two young drivers hoping to make it big—always looking to the other to best gauge their own progress.

Now Stewart's rival is gone, and his trip back to the scene of Irwin's death will always be bittersweet.

Stewart won at New Hampshire International Speedway last July, just a few days after Irwin was killed after crashing into the wall on Turn 3 during practice. A fitting tribute, indeed, but hardly an occasion to celebrate.

"Any win in the Winston Cup Series is big. But with the tragedy of losing Kenny, to lose him like that, it just made it even more important to win the race in his memory."

—Tony Stewart

"Any win in the Winston Cup Series is big," Stewart said. "But with the tragedy of losing Kenny, to lose him like that, it just made it even more important to win the race in his memory."

Their careers took remarkably similar paths.

A couple of Indiana boys, they began competing in 1991 in the open-wheel U.S. Auto Club sprint series, where they engaged in a heated race for Rookie of the Year.

Stewart won that battle, but the rivalry was only beginning. It continued in different USAC series through 1996, when Irwin joined the NASCAR Craftsman Truck Series and Stewart went to the Indy Racing League.

Irwin moved to Winston Cup in 1998 and was Rookie of the Year. The rivalry was renewed a year later when Stewart got the call to Winston Cup from Joe Gibbs and followed Irwin as the best rookie of 1999.

In their first year on the Winston Cup circuit together, they had a flare-up—the tempestuous Stewart throwing heat shields from his shoes at Irwin after the two collided twice at a race in Martinsville, Va.

They were never best of friends.

"Through nine years of rivalry, there's been a mutual admiration and respect for one another and for what each other could do in a race car," Stewart said. "I've said this a thousand times since I started in Winston Cup: Kenny's part of the reason I got here, because he pushed me to make myself better each week."

Naturally, Stewart isn't alone in his mixed feelings about returning to Loudon.

Kyle Petty, whose son Adam died here six weeks before Irwin, was holding out until a few hours before qualifying begins Friday to decide whether he would make the trip. If he doesn't, Steve Grissom will likely take his spot in the No. 45 car.

The rest of the field will be here, also with some obvious reservations.

Very little at this track has changed since the Petty and Irwin tragedies: Loudon still has long straightaways, very little banking, and tight, unforgiving corners. It was a formula ripe for tragedy last year, when Petty and Irwin both apparently encountered stuck throttles and slammed into the wall.

Last September—when the series returned to New Hampshire for the first time after the tragedies— NASCAR mandated restrictor plates to slow speeds. It was a response to an outcry from drivers who felt some safety measures had to be taken at a track where two people died in the span of six weeks.

This year, the restrictor-plate requirement has been lifted.

"There are some other things we've done to the cars that has helped slow down the speeds," said NASCAR president Mike Helton, speaking mainly of new suspension rules that make the cars ride differently than last year.

Helton also pointed to a relatively tame Busch race in May as proof that the track is still functional without restrictor plates.

"It's not really the race track," Bobby Labonte said. "That can happen anywhere. Now, with the race track being flat and 3,400-pound cars trying to go around it two-wide, that isn't necessarily the best mix as far as racing. But it's not the race track."

Others, like Jeff Burton, disagree.

"I'm sure people feel better about what they're doing inside their car, but there has been nothing that's been made better for the race track," he said.

It seems every safety-related issue has been subject to debate in the 14 months since Petty's death began a string of four fatalities within NASCAR's ranks, including Tony Roper and Dale Earnhardt.

Like racing itself, those debates go on without Stewart's old rival, Irwin, whose name will always be linked to the tragedy at New Hampshire.

"It's just a hard thing to deal with," Stewart said. "I still think I'm going to walk around a corner and he is going to be there somewhere."

"The thing about Tony is, he's a racer. How do you tell somebody is a racer? That's hard to explain. But you either are or you aren't."

—Scott Diehl, Joe Gibbs Racing

STEWART FORGIVES AND FORGETS HIS WAY TO VICTORY

By JENNA FRYER, AP Sports Writer

August 25, 2001

BRISTOL, Tenn. (AP)—The situation had the potential for disaster: Jeff Gordon leading lap after lap around the tight turns of Bristol with hot-headed Tony Stewart right on his bumper.

The two clashed in this very place just a few months before, and the slightest tap from Stewart could have sent his rival into the wall and been the sweetest redemption.

Instead, Stewart slipped right past Gordon and drove off to victory in Saturday night's Sharpie 500—proving he can forgive and forget.

"There are 43 professional guys that start the race every week and you're not going to get along with all of them 100 percent of the time," Stewart said. "Bristol in the spring was Bristol in the spring; this is the fall race. It's a whole different day."

Still, it's doubtful retaliation was far from Stewart's mind as he followed Gordon around and around Bristol Motor Speedway.

After all, it was initial contact from Gordon in the spring race that started a chain of events that have marred Stewart's season.

He was running fourth in the final turn of that race when Gordon, charging hard behind him as the two headed to the finish line, sent him into a spin as he tried to pass him. Stewart's car went shooting up the high banking, missing the wall by mere inches.

By the time Stewart refired his car and made it back to the line, he had fallen 21 spots behind and finished 25th. Incensed, he stalked Gordon around the track, catching him on pit road and bumping him out of his way.

The action drew a $10,000 fine and landed Stewart on probation—which should have ended this month had it not been extended for the rest of the year after an outburst at Daytona in July.

Because of how lightly Stewart must tread these days, Gordon never worried about possible revenge.

"Why would I worry?" Gordon said before the race. "He's on probation."

In the end, it was Stewart's desire to win on his favorite track that took priority.

Although he came into the race with 11 career victories, none of them were at Bristol Motor Speedway—a track he liked before he even drove stock cars and fell in love with the minute he saw it.

"The first time I came in here I was amazed; we came through that gate and got down into the infield, I looked up and never saw a sight like what I saw that day," Stewart said. "Anytime anybody has ever asked me what my favorite track was, I always say Bristol."

That's a strong statement from the Indiana native, who has gone to great lengths in an attempt to fulfill his childhood dream of winning the Indianapolis 500. He never has, notching a career-best finish of sixth in May.

If winning there would be his greatest triumph, winning at Bristol was his most satisfying victory.

"Having the opportunity to drink the milk in Victory Lane [at Indy] is something I dearly hope I have an opportunity to do before I quit driving race cars," he said. "This is just one of those places where the style of racing is what I enjoy.

"That's what probably makes it so satisfying to win here—the way you have to be aggressive and you have to at the same time be patient and stay out of all the wrecks all day and work lapped traffic. It makes it more gratifying when you can do that at a place like this."

For a long while, it didn't look like Stewart would be able to chase down Gordon or continuously avoid the race-record 16 cautions.

Every time Stewart chipped into Gordon's lead, his work was erased by yet another yellow flag. Gordon was far superior on the restarts but lacked the car to hold off Stewart on long runs.

When Stewart finally caught a break with 30 uninterrupted laps, he passed Gordon with a sweeping slide that started on the bottom of the track in Turn 2 and finished in Turn 4 on Lap 432.

"When Tony got to me I knew it was just a matter of time," Gordon said. "We just got beat; he was real good on the long runs. I think maybe what we needed was some more cautions, because when we ran real long, my car got tight and Tony was really good."

But caution never came out again, and Gordon was not a factor the rest of the way. Stewart needed only to hold off rookie Kevin Harvick for his third victory of the season.

"It's just awesome to win at Bristol; it's so hard to do," Stewart said. "So many things happen and there are so many things that can go wrong, and I'm just glad we were able to do it."

"I believe this in my heart: I've worked as hard, and gone through as much, and made as many sacrifices as anybody in Winston Cup racing today. That's why I am the way I am, and that's why I say the things I say."

—Tony Stewart

STEWART MAKES NOISE, HEARS PLENTY

By JENNA FRYER, AP Sports Writer

September 5, 2001

The loud booing began the second Tony Stewart hit the stage at driver introductions. He smiled and waved to the crowd, hiding his deep disappointment behind dark sunglasses.

The negative reaction doesn't compare to the vicious booing Jeff Gordon receives, but the three-time Winston Cup champion deals with it. Try as he might, Stewart can't get beyond it.

"I hate it and I can't understand it," he said. "The last thing I want to do before I get in a car is go through driver introductions and hear half the place booing me. It makes me wonder what I've done to make them hate me so much, and it's a difficult thing to be the last thing you hear before the race."

There's a sensitive side to Stewart, a fiery and short-fused 30-year-old driver as well known for tantrums and bad behavior as he is for being the best rookie in history and accumulating 12 career victories in fewer than three seasons on the circuit.

There's a notion among fans that he and Gordon are bitter rivals, fueled mostly by a trio of on-track confrontations.

Stewart has been branded the bad guy of the story line, earning him angry receptions from Gordon loyalists. When he spun Gordon out on pit road at Bristol Motor Speedway in March—an action that drew him a $10,000 fine and six months on probation—the hatred toward Stewart accelerated.

In truth, the rivalry between the two is virtually nonexistent.

"Tony and I have no problems with each other; we just race one another hard and we've gotten into one another a couple of times," Gordon said. "A guy as good and strong as Tony, you're going to battle with him a lot.

"I think we have a lot of respect for each other, and our fans probably rival one another far more than anything else."

Then there's Stewart's icy relationship with the media, spurred on by his sarcasm and candor. When Stewart believes he is being genuine and honest, he's often received as being rude and arrogant.

He insists he doesn't mean to come across that way.

"The way things are these days is you're supposed to say the right things and be sweet and charming, but I don't know anything about racing that's sweet and charming," he said. "People think I don't care, but what they're missing is that I actually care too much.

"People think I'm just an angry, mean person. But I'm not—I'm just frustrated because I try to make everybody happy and I can't, no matter what I do."

The two situations have created a sadness Stewart can't hide and a mounting frustration that has him feeling as if he's walking on eggshells.

When not in the car, he spends much of his time at the track these days holed up in his trailer or motor home, scared that when he comes out he'll do or say something to offend someone.

J. D. Gibbs, president of Joe Gibbs Racing, said that might be the best thing for him right now.

"We've talked to him and said he's taking so much heat,

let's just take a step back and let it blow over," Gibbs said. "And it will; people forget if you just treat them right and with respect. Right now, he just has to be careful."

There's a carry-over onto the track, where he fears aggressive actions could get him into even more trouble with NASCAR. On probation for the rest of the year—punishment for ignoring a black flag at Daytona in July, then angrily confronting a reporter and a NASCAR official—Stewart could be suspended for another infraction.

"I'm scared to walk through the garage area and have one of my shoelaces be untied because I'm going to make somebody mad with it," he said. "I'm scared to death of touching Jeff Gordon because if I do, then all his fans who already don't like me, what are they going to do to me next?"

If it sounds as if Stewart is looking for sympathy, he's not.

He understands he's judged by his infractions, but firmly defends his actions.

Hitting Gordon on pit road? That was payback for the spin Gordon sent him into minutes before. Vehemently arguing about the black flag? He has a right to his opinion and believed he was being unfairly penalized.

Looking back, he regrets nothing. If he could change it, he'd learn to be a better liar.

"If those things make me a bad guy, then yeah, I guess I'm a bad guy," Stewart said. "Before now, I'd never once gotten in trouble for defending myself or for arguing what I believe to be a valid point. So I guess I better learn to start saying what everyone wants to hear rather than the truth."

Gordon, whose mouth rarely gets him in trouble, thinks that might be a good approach for Stewart.

"Sometimes he says some things that get him in trouble," Gordon said. "That's kind of caught Tony, unfortunately, in a bad situation. Tony is probably a much better guy than people perceive him to be"

Home Depot, the sponsor of the Pontiac Stewart drives for Joe Gibbs Racing, also believes the non-racing problems have spoiled the driver's reputation.

"He is so genuine, and because of that, the way he naturally reacts to adversity has been his stumbling

"The way things are these days is you're supposed to say the right things and be sweet and charming, but I don't know anything about racing that's sweet and charming."

—Tony Stewart

block," said Hugh Miskel, who oversees Home Depot's racing program. "We'd like to help him in better reacting to situations, because Tony has a little bit of a feeling like he has been wronged. If he learned to deal with that in a little more healthy of a manner it would be good for him personally and professionally."

If this were another day and time, none of this would be an issue.

Stewart grew up idolizing A. J. Foyt, a Texan with a famous temper who could throw a punch as easily as he could pass a compliment. And there was a time in stock car racing when drivers fought after accidents and constantly criticized NASCAR.

Stewart, perhaps a throwback to those days, understands times have changed. He doesn't like it, but is learning to accept it.

"I know things can't continue the way they are," he said. "I'd like for things not to bother me so much and I'd like to be able to tune everything out. I'm working on it, I really am."

"I ran one lap, pulled in and bailed out of the car because I felt like I was getting trapped inside the car. It was because of my own anxiety that comes from being claustrophobic. That's how the HANS device makes me feel."

—Tony Stewart

STEWART UNEASY ABOUT HEAD-AND-NECK RESTRAINTS

By JENNA FRYER, AP Sports Writer

October 18, 2001

TALLADEGA, Ala. (AP)—Tony Stewart no longer has any choice about wearing a head-and-neck restraint, and that makes him uneasy.

A new rule forcing drivers to wear either a HANS or Hutchens device begins with qualifying Friday for the EA Sports 500 at Talladega Superspeedway, one of the most dangerous tracks in NASCAR.

Stewart is NASCAR's lone holdout on trying such restraints, citing claustrophobia and questions about their effectiveness. The mandate now takes the issue out of his hands, and Stewart isn't very happy about it.

"I want to wear something, but I haven't found anything yet that I'm comfortable with," he said. "It's not that I don't want to wear it, and I'm not being bullheaded about this, but there is nothing right now that I'm comfortable wearing inside the race car."

Before Wednesday, the use of a restraint system was encouraged by NASCAR but not required. Still, 42 of 43 drivers routinely wore one of the two available devices—a factor NASCAR said played a part in the mandate.

Widespread use of the devices, which limit movement of a driver's head and neck upon impact, began shortly after seven-time Winston Cup champion Dale Earnhardt died of a fractured skull in the season-opening Daytona 500. Neither Earnhardt nor three other NASCAR drivers who died of head or neck injuries in the preceding nine months was wearing a restraining device.

Because of his claustrophobia, the bulky, over-the-shoulder HANS device has never been an option for Stewart. He tried the less-cumbersome Hutchens device one time during a testing session at Talladega in August, but he was bothered by it and grew suspicious of its reliability when the series of straps and buckles were attached to his body a different way each of the three times he got into the car.

He found its presence a distraction and decided that wasn't a safe state of mind to have when driving at speeds close to 190 mph.

Stewart had a similar problem when he once tried a foam headrest in an open-wheel car. The headrest sat on the rim of the driver's cockpit and slightly touched the top of his shoulders—still too much of a distraction for him.

"I ran one lap, pulled in and bailed out of the car because I felt like I was getting trapped inside the car," he said. "It was because of my own anxiety that comes from being claustrophobic. That's how the HANS device makes me feel."

NASCAR said it tried several times in the past few days to contact Stewart and discuss the mandate with him, finally calling car owner Joe Gibbs to explain its decision.

"We expect them to comply with the rules," said NASCAR vice president George Pyne. "Joe understands what we are trying to do and that it is the right thing for our industry, which Tony is a big part of. We fully expect that Tony will race this weekend with the device on."

But Pyne admitted NASCAR has no penalty on the books yet should Stewart fail to comply with the mandate. And there's always the possibility that the independent and outspoken Stewart could attempt to get into his car without one of the restraints.

Talladega is not a place where Stewart needs any kind of distraction. At 2.66 miles, the high-banked oval is the longest and fastest track on the circuit. The field is typically bunched together for the entire 500 miles, meaning he should already be on edge from the bumper-to-bumper racing.

The discomfort from a new safety device could heighten that.

"If I have a helmet device that doesn't fit properly or isn't comfortable, then how comfortable am I going to be six inches from guys who are on all four corners of my race car?" he asked.

Jeff Burton, an active participant in the push for safety in NASCAR, had some sympathy for Stewart's plight but still thinks the restraints are the right thing.

"I really wish that NASCAR didn't have to do something like this where they had to mandate drivers to wear a safety device," Burton said. "People should take the initiative to try and make it safer for themselves."

"I think his intensity is his best friend and it's his enemy at the same time. There is nobody out there who is more talented, and I don't think there is anybody out there who is more capable of winning races and championships."

—Jeff Gordon

STEWART PUTS TURBULENT 2001 BEHIND HIM

By JENNA FRYER, AP Sports Writer

January 16, 2002

Tony Stewart started last season by flipping his Pontiac down the backstretch in a wreck at the Daytona 500. It set the tone of a turbulent year of penalties, probation, politics—and, oh yeah, a career-best second-place finish in the standings.

With a new season set to begin, the slate is supposedly wiped clean. But with Stewart, one never can tell if it has been.

The biggest questions surrounding Stewart this season are: Can he forget about last year's tumultuous times? And can he effectively learn how to manage his time—and his temper—in the future?

If the answers are "yes," then 2001 series champion Jeff Gordon thinks Stewart is probably the top contender to take his title away.

"I think his intensity is his best friend and it's his enemy at the same time," Gordon said. "There is nobody out there who is more talented, and I don't think there is anybody out there who is more capable of winning races and championships.

"But I definitely see where there are things that get in the way of the focus at times."

Stewart understands that people believe his own temper and occasional lack of focus are the two biggest speed bumps blocking the path to his first-ever Winston Cup championship.

But he doesn't believe it and points to the numerous championships he's won on other circuits—most recently the 1997 Indy Racing League title—as proof.

"If you win races, you can win a championship, that's the way I look at," Stewart said. "It's not rocket science, there's no theories behind it. The guy who is the most consistent all year wins at the end."

Stewart, who set the mark as the most successful rookie

> **"If you win races, you can win a championship, that's the way I look at it. It's not rocket science, there's no theories behind it. The guy who is the most consistent all year wins at the end."**
>
> —Tony Stewart

in NASCAR history in 1999, has proven he can win races by racking up 12 victories in three seasons.

But he's developed a reputation as a hot-head who stands in his own way.

Last year alone, he spun out Gordon on pit road, argued with a Winston Cup official after an on-track penalty, and knocked a tape recorder from a reporter's hands after the confrontation.

He butted heads with NASCAR over the required use of head-and-neck restraints and battled with the media and fans for the demands on his time.

He racked up $20,000 in fines, spent most of the year on probation and alienated many people.

"It was a tough year," he admitted. "But it's over. And all I can try to do is learn from it, look at any mistakes I might have made and try to grow from them."

There's still some things that Stewart never changes.

When at the track, Stewart doesn't want be bothered. Not by reporters seeking one of his always candid and usually a little colorful quotes, not by photographers quick to snap up a familiar scowl, and not by the bold fan who daringly asks for an autograph.

He understands everyone has a job to do and wishes they'd understand that he does, too.

It's not as though Stewart doesn't try to do both. Although he was one of the chief complainers last year about the length of the season and how draining it was, he's taken almost no time off this winter to recharge.

One of the busiest drivers on the circuit, Stewart limited himself to one break—a five-day trip to the Bahamas in December—and estimated it was his first vacation since he was a young child.

Then it was off to appearances, autograph sessions, test sessions, sponsor obligations and the many other races he squeezes into his schedule, leaving him with roughly five free days before he heads to Daytona next month for the start of the season.

It doesn't stop then, either. He visits an average of 25 Home Depot stores all over the country during the season, meeting the associates who sponsor his Joe Gibbs Racing car and greeting the fans who line up outside the store hours before his scheduled arrival.

And he tries to remain true to his short track roots, racing in about 35 other events a year aside from NASCAR. He's also a hands-on owner for his sprint car team, which won the World of Outlaws championship in its first season.

At every stop, he shows the charm and personality that is often lost at the track.

He spent a recent afternoon laughing and joking with a camera crew that was shooting a video of him answering trivia questions that will be used on his souvenir truck at the tracks.

He slipped into a phony Italian accent when talking about crew chief Greg Zipadelli and came up with quips and one-liners to answer other questions.

Stewart tried to show NASCAR that side of him at its annual awards ceremony in December. Midway through his nationally televised speech, Stewart removed his tuxedo jacket to reveal a head-and-neck restraint he'd been wearing all night as a way to poke fun at his earlier reluctance to wear one.

The prank drew rousing applause and hearty laughs from NASCAR's brass.

"Everything I heard about that was positive," Stewart said. "People didn't know I could be funny, but I can be. I'm not a bad guy, I just want to win and do my job.

"If I was always relaxed and having fun and joking with the fans, I bet I wouldn't be a very good race car driver."

"In my lifetime there's probably been only two or three guys I've known who could drive just about anything they sat down in, and Tony Stewart is one of 'em."

—A. J. Foyt

DEFENDING CHAMPION STEWART CHERISHES SHOOTOUT VICTORY

By JENNA FRYER, AP Sports Writer

February 8, 2002

DAYTONA BEACH, Fla. (AP)—Of all the victories Tony Stewart has accumulated over his career, outdueling Dale Earnhardt in last year's Budweiser Shootout ranks as one of his greatest thrills.

Using every blocking move he could and his limited drafting experience, Stewart held off Earnhardt—the master of restrictor-plate racing—over the final two laps of the made-for-TV event at Daytona International Speedway.

The victory was Stewart's first-ever on a superspeedway, earned him a $202,000 payout and gave him a sense of pride in one-upping Earnhardt at what

he did best. The seven-time Winston Cup champion was killed a week later in a wreck on the final lap of the Daytona 500.

"It was cool the day that I won, beating Dale at his own game, that gave you the respect that you were looking for," Stewart said. "And after we lost Dale, it made that win so much more special. I'd much rather be here to try to duplicate that race with him again this year."

Stewart will attempt to defend his title in the 70-lap event held Sunday and generally considered a brief preview of the Daytona 500.

The field for the non-points race is made up of pole winners from last season and former event champions, with a record 22 drivers included this year. The winner will receive at least $200,000 of the $966,000 purse and some confidence to take into the Feb. 17 season-opening 500.

"The entire team is heading in there with a go-for-broke attitude," Stewart said. "There aren't any points involved. It's just money, a trophy and a lot of prestige."

It also gives the 22 drivers involved a slight edge over the other teams here, because they get extra track time to prepare for the 500. They'll get a chance to test NASCAR's new aerodynamic package while working on drafting and strategy.

"The Bud Shootout is a huge advantage for the guys who are in it," four-time series champion Jeff Gordon said. "You really don't get into any situations during practice. You can try, but you really don't get race conditions until the Shootout. I'm looking at it as getting a race under my belt that I can play around with some stuff and see what you need to do to move through the field."

Gordon will have plenty of opportunity—he starts in the back of the field, which was set Thursday by blind draw. Kurt Busch will start from the pole, with Kenny Wallace on the outside of the front row.

Jason Leffler, who lost his ride at the end of last season, qualified for the event by winning a pole last year but could not find a car to enter in the race and is the only eligible driver not competing.

TONY STEWART

"It's been a long time coming here for me. Bobby always has a lot of luck here. I'm sorry he didn't have good luck today."

—Tony Stewart

STEWART HOLDS OFF EARNHARDT FOR ATLANTA VICTORY

By KEITH PARSONS, AP Sports Writer

March 10, 2002

HAMPTON, Ga. (AP)—His second straight dominating performance wasn't enough to convince Tony Stewart his Pontiac is on equal footing.

Stewart slid under Ward Burton for the lead with 24 laps to go and held off Dale Earnhardt Jr. to win the MBNA America 500 at Atlanta Motor Speedway on Sunday. It was Stewart's 13th career victory.

One of NASCAR's most outspoken drivers, Stewart has complained all year about the aerodynamic disadvantages of his manufacturer. He didn't have any problems Sunday, leading the most laps for the second straight race to get his first victory of the season. He beat Earnhardt by about five car lengths.

But he wasn't ready to stop asking for help.

"Not if you sat in the car with me in fourth or fifth spot behind a bunch of cars," Stewart said. "Just like last week, when we were out in clean air, we were fast."

The decisive pass came in Turn 1, when Stewart moved to the inside and slid in front of Burton. It was similar to the "slide-job" passes Stewart used throughout his sprint car days, although most of those were on dirt.

This was on pavement and at 190 mph.

"I had four or five of those today," Stewart said of the technique. "You have to know where their weak spot is on the race track. The biggest thing was, even if I had to check up when I got in front of him, I just had to get in front."

After a 43rd-place finish in the season-opening Daytona 500, Stewart has finished in the top five in three straight races and climbed back into the points race. He's now fifth, 101 points behind leader Sterling Marlin, who finished ninth.

> ## "It's been a long time coming here for me."
> ### —Tony Stewart

The final pass was the 34th lead change of the day, a record for this race, although the finish didn't match the past two in this event. Kevin Harvick beat Jeff Gordon by .006 seconds last year, and the late Dale Earnhardt edged Bobby Labonte by .01 two years ago.

Earnhardt took second from Burton with 22 laps left and immediately began closing on Stewart by using a different line. With Stewart running on the bottom of the track, Earnhardt moved up a lane and got within two car lengths.

But Stewart adjusted his line and began pulling away.

"I moved up the race track and it seemed to help my car, and I thought I might catch him," Earnhardt said. "But he moved up to the same line the next lap. He's a smart race car driver."

Rookie Jimmie Johnson continued his surprising start, finishing third. Matt Kenseth, forced to start at the rear because he changed engines after qualifying, placed fourth. Ricky Craven was fifth.

The competition at the front of the field was tight all day, with at least five cars in the hunt.

"It's always fun running here," Earnhardt said. "This race track always has good racing. You can make an attempt to pass a guy in almost every corner. I love racing here."

NASCAR's new one-engine rule seemed to have dramatic effect, with at least seven cars experiencing engine problems, including Harvick's and Michael Waltrip's.

Labonte, Stewart's teammate for Joe Gibbs Racing and a winner as this track five times since 1996, fell off the pace with a dropped cylinder.

"It's been a long time coming here for me," Stewart said. "Bobby always has a lot of luck here. I'm sorry he didn't have good luck today."

Johnson, who finished sixth last week at Las Vegas, steadily charged through the field after starting 15th. He was closing on the top two at the checkered flag.

"I thought a couple of times there we might have a shot to win," Johnson said. "It just blows my mind that we've been this competitive this early."

"If I put on a game face as a race approaches, it's because I know what I'm there for. I always have."

—Tony Stewart

A PATIENT STEWART RULES AGAIN AT RICHMOND

By HANK KURZ Jr., AP Sports Writer

May 5, 2002

RICHMOND, Va. (AP)—Tony Stewart has no idea why he rules Richmond International Raceway.

He has three victories in seven career starts at the track and has finished in the top 10 in three of the other races.

"I don't have any secrets here," he said after pulling away from Ryan Newman on a restart with 17 laps to go Sunday to win the rain-delayed Pontiac Excitement 400. "I guess I just get around here good."

The victory was Stewart's second of the season and 14th of his career.

"I probably ran one of the most patient races I've ever run," he said. "And it wasn't because I wanted to but because I had to."

There were a track record-tying 14 caution periods and a record 103 laps run under the yellow flag on the track billed "The Action Track."

"There were a lot of guys that were being very courteous, a lot of give and take going on out there," he said. "And then there were a lot of guys that were in a big hurry, and it seemed like the guys that got in a hurry, sure enough, as time went on they were dropping out like flies."

Stewart's car wasn't cooperating early, but crew chief Greg Zipadelli kept the faith.

"Greg will listen to me whine and carry on on the radio and he'll let me get depressed," Stewart said. "Then he'll come back and start pumping me up and the next thing you know, we're back where we need to be."

The victory lifted Stewart from 10th to eighth in the points race and came from the back of the field. He qualified third but had to change motors after qualifying and was penalized, going to the back of the field.

He was 27th when the race resumed for the final 334 laps after what amounted to a 14-hour rain delay and gradually worked his way forward.

He passed Mark Martin for third with 67 laps to go, got by Jeff Gordon for second with 55 laps left and then set his sights on Newman, a rookie who ran in the top five all day and was strongest on long runs.

After following on Newman's bumper for several laps, Stewart finally sneaked his car underneath on the 372nd lap, rode side by side with Newman for a lap and then pulled ahead for good entering the first turn.

Newman held on for second in his Ford, followed by the Fords of Jack Roush teammates Jeff Burton and Martin and Jeremy Mayfield's Dodge.

"From the drop of the green flag last night to the checkered flag today, we knew we had a good car," Newman said. "We had a car that was capable of winning, but sometimes you can't finish what you start."

Count Stewart among those impressed by Newman.

"He is probably the smartest, most calculated young driver we have in our series right now and he's not got his win yet," Stewart said. "But a day like today, when you lose it in the last 20 laps, is the day that really makes you appreciate it when you do get that first win."

Burton, meanwhile, rallied for his best finish of the season after cutting a tire with about 100 laps to go.

NASCAR
Winston Cup
Series
NASCAR
Winston Cup
Series
Tony Stewart

"I think we came out 28th with about 100 laps to go and drove up to third, so that was all we had," he said. "That was all we could get."

Matt Kenseth, another Roush driver, came from three laps down early to finish sixth, and Jeff Gordon finished seventh as the top Chevrolet.

For much of the day, it looked as if Ricky Rudd would make history in style in his record-tying 655th consecutive start. He led 90 laps and seemed to have the dominant car until he crashed with 91 laps to go.

Marlin finished 11th and remained the points leader. He is 132 ahead of Kenseth, who passed Kurt Busch for second. Busch is third, 191 behind, and Martin is fourth, giving Roush three of the top four. Martin is 193 back.

"It doesn't matter what he does, Tony is exhausted when he's done. I think it's because he puts 100 percent into everything he does. I mean if you go against him on a go-kart track, he'll put 100 percent into that go-kart track."

—Bob Burris, Tony Stewart Racing

NO DOUBLE DUTY FOR STEWART

By JENNA FRYER, AP Sports Writer

May 25, 2002

CONCORD, N.C. (AP)—With a chance at winning a $1 million bonus and improving his position in the points standings, Tony Stewart decided one race was enough for him.

Stewart chose not to compete in both the Indianapolis 500 and the Coca-Cola 600 on Sunday, a double-duty event he has done twice before.

Instead, he'll focus only on his NASCAR job, avoiding all the hassles that go with "double duty." A year ago, he had to have a specialized diet to get ready for the physical demands of the 1,100 miles of racing. He also had to follow a detailed schedule to help with all the travel logistics.

> "I'm actually happy about the position we're in the point standings right now. I would much rather be the hunter than the hunted right now."
>
> —Tony Stewart

Robby Gordon is running in both races, competing in Indianapolis in the day, then rushing to Lowe's Motor Speedway for the evening start. Mike Wallace will be on standby in case Gordon misses the start.

Eliminating all of that helps Stewart's chances of winning the 600.

"We don't want to take a chance on doing anything that could jeopardize those chances for us," Stewart said. "We feel like this is our best opportunity to win a championship. Our performance on the track has been good enough to do that. We just need a little luck on our side."

Stewart heads into Sunday's race—the longest of the season—ranked eighth in the points standings. He's got two victories but believes he should have more and be much higher in the standings.

He was considered a heavy favorite at the season-opening Daytona 500 but blew a motor two laps into the race. He was injured in a wreck while leading at Darlington, hurting his back to the point where he had to get out of his car the next week at Bristol, even though he was headed toward a strong finish.

He made the decision to skip Indy, a title the former open-wheel star and Indiana native has always coveted, because this is his best chance to dominate in NASCAR. An added incentive is the $1 million bonus he and four others are eligible for if they win the Coca-Cola 600.

Stewart finished a career-best third in this event last year after finishing sixth at Indy.

"It seems like, historically, in the past, this is the part of the year where we'll really start getting on a run and get some consistent top fives and hopefully some more wins here pretty soon," he said.

"I'm actually happy about the position we're in the point standings right now. I would much rather be the hunter than the hunted right now."

> "We don't want to take a chance on doing anything that could jeopardize those chances for us. We feel like this is our best opportunity to win a championship. Our performance on the track has been good enough to do that. We just need a little luck on our side."
>
> —Tony Stewart

High Octane in the Fast Lane

"*There have been times in some of my very best races when I muscled the car around more than I should have, getting really aggressive when I didn't need to. But I was having so much fun that I had to keep on pushing it, pushing myself. I was in that zone.*"

—Tony Stewart

STEWART STILL HEARS BOOS, BUT NOT AS MANY

By DICK BRINSTER, AP Sports Writer

June 12, 2002

Tony Stewart steps forward, waves to the crowd and gets his usual greeting.

"Boooooooooooooooo!"

It's just NASCAR fans venting at one of their favorite villains.

But lately, Stewart has been hearing some cheers, too, giving him the feeling that things may be changing.

"The booing isn't as bad as it used to be," he said. "But it's still there."

And that's fine with Stewart, whose next chance to hear the crowd will be Sunday at Michigan Speedway.

"I think if we totally lose the boos, that's got to be a bad sign," he said. "It means we're doing something wrong."

Four-time Winston Cup champion Jeff Gordon, who still gets the big thumbs-down from the crowd, shares that feeling.

"Dale Earnhardt once told me that when they stop booing, you better start worrying," Gordon has said.

Stewart believes his team draws boos because it's a constant threat to beat the popular drivers.

"That shows that we're doing things right," he said.

Few have done better, from a record-setting 1999 rookie season through 14 career victories.

Still, it's been a rough ride. Stewart has drawn fines and probation from NASCAR for his behavior, he outraged fans with complaints that too many of them are in the garage area, making the teams' jobs more difficult, and he had to explain that he wasn't trying to insult Alabama when was quoted in a British magazine as saying that Talladega had the most obnoxious fans.

He has spent a lot of time apologizing, repenting or denying.

No more. Once the most accessible driver on the Winston Cup circuit, he has slammed the door on most of the media.

"Now I'm enjoying myself from Monday through Thursday instead of running around covering my tracks, doing damage control because somebody didn't agree with something I said," he added.

How long will this continue?

"Until people show us that things are different and you can actually speak your mind without repercussions," he said, speaking softly and in a controlled fashion—hardly the loud and disorderly image that many have of him.

He still loses his temper, but this season, it's been mostly in private.

Frustrations are aired to crew chief Greg Zipadelli, car owner Joe Gibbs or others close to him. There, Stewart said, he's "allowed to be a person."

"In this day and age, a personality is a bad thing to have in Winston Cup racing," he said. "If you have one, you're in trouble."

Stewart rarely has trouble communicating with Zipadelli. Both are obsessed with winning, and even a minor skid is a concern.

Earlier this month, they failed to contend at Dover International Speedway, one of the circuit's most difficult tracks. Stewart swept the races there in 2000 and had never finished worse than seventh in six starts. He wound up 11th in a car Zipadelli thought was far worse than that. But they didn't congratulate themselves.

"I'm not proud of an 11th-place finish," Zipadelli said. "I'm ashamed and embarrassed."

Still, Stewart is sixth in the series standings and shares the lead with two wins. That's not good enough for Stewart or Zipadelli, but they realize their aging Pontiac is no match for the Chevrolets, Fords or Dodges.

"We're going to Michigan, and it will be the same dang thing again," Zipadelli said after a seventh-place finish Sunday at Pocono Raceway.

Joe Gibbs Racing is weighing the use of a redesigned Pontiac against switching next season to a Chevrolet. Stewart, who feels loyalty to Pontiac, wants no role in that decision.

He established himself early as a racing talent on the short tracks of the Midwest, became a USAC champion, won a title in the IRL and quickly became a major force in NASCAR.

Like him or not, his high profile has been good for business. He does commercials for The Home Depot, Pontiac and others with racing interests and says his souvenir sales are the best they've been in three years.

In part, he credits his new book, *True Speed*, for making the ride with fans a little smoother.

"It gives people an opportunity to see who I am, why I do the things I do and say the things I say," Stewart said.

"But a race is a race. If five other guys show up, I want to beat those five guys; if it's fifty other guys, same thing. And if I can't beat them all, I'll get as many as I can."

—Tony Stewart

DEFENDING CHAMP STEWART EARNS POLE AT SEARS POINT

By ANNE M. PETERSON, AP Sports Writer

June 21 , 2002

SONOMA, Calif. (AP)—Tony Stewart has a plan. He won't pay attention to Jeff Gordon—unless Gordon is directly in front of him or right behind.

"I never worry about anybody after that," Stewart said. "You've got to race each person one at a time."

Gordon may be the road course king, but Stewart reigns for the moment at Sears Point.

Stewart took the first step toward defending his title in the Dodge/Save Mart 350 by winning the pole on Friday.

He had not won a pole in 58 races, dating to Martinsville Speedway nearly two years ago. At Sears Point last year, he qualified with third.

Stewart's lap of 93.476 mph on the scenic wine country course also gave Pontiac its first pole of the season for Sunday's race.

Kurt Busch went from a provisional entry last year to the second best qualifier this year with a lap of 93.184. Fellow Ford driver Jeff Burton beat four-time Winston Cup champion Jeff Gordon with a lap of 93.166.

Gordon went 93.141 mph in a new, specially designed Chevrolet Monte Carlo.

He has won at Sears Point three of the last four years and holds the NASCAR record with seven career road course victories. He is flattered other drivers think he's the guy to beat at Sears Point and at Watkins Glen, the only other road course on the Winston Cup schedule.

"That's a compliment," Gordon said. "We have certainly been real strong out here, won a lot of races, and won a lot of races on these road courses and have been the guy to beat."

Burton, who will have his second top-10 start of the year on Sunday, kept it simple on the 10-turn, two-mile track.

"What's made me a better road course driver is just

driving the darn thing," he said. "Just drive like a teenager when you're parents aren't watching."

Bill Elliott rounded out the top five with a lap of 93.116 in his Dodge.

In nine career starts at Sears Point, Gordon has three wins, three poles, six top five finishes and seven top 10s.

Last year, Gordon had the pole for the race and led the first 32 laps. But Stewart, who qualified third, slipped under Robby Gordon while exiting the track's famed Chute and led the final 10 laps for the win.

He's qualified well at Sears Point, starting second in 1999, fourth in 2000 and then third last year. Four times the pole winner has gone on to capture Sears Point.

"It's not so much of an advantage, but it gives the drivers a little more of a luxury of taking care of their cars," Stewart said. "They're not working hard to get to the front. They're already there. So they don't have to abuse their brakes, they don't have to abuse their tires."

Dale Jarrett chose not to qualify after experiencing problems with his Ford in the morning practice. That means he'll be a provisional entry with a 37th-place start.

Jarrett, who had the pole last weekend in Brooklyn, Mich., said the problem began with the oil pump, and he eventually had to change engines.

"This track has changed," Jarrett said. "And with me not having made a full lap, we decided to sit tight and get ready for practice in the morning."

"My dream of winning the Indy 500 is no less intense today than it ever was. It's still the race. It's still the goal. And as long as I feel this passionately about it, I guess I might as well keep after it."

—Tony Stewart

BRICKYARD 400: PRESSURE BUILDS AS INDIANA'S STEWART WINS POLE

By MIKE HARRIS, The Associated Press

August 3, 2002

INDIANAPOLIS—The way Tony Stewart likes to handle pressure is to get in his race car and drive—fast.

He did that yesterday, ignoring the oppressive heat, overcoming a slick track and shaking off a myriad of outside distractions to win the pole for the Brickyard 400 today.

Stewart, an Indiana native, sat in the window of his Joe Gibbs Pontiac and pumped his fists in the air, taking in the booming cheers of the partisan crowd of about 30,000 after setting a track qualifying record.

His lap at 182.960 mph easily broke the record of 181.072,

set in 2000 by Brett Bodine. The top five qualifiers surpassed that speed despite temperatures in the 90s and a glaring sun that made the 2.5-mile asphalt oval treacherous.

Stewart, who grew up about 30 miles from Indianapolis Motor Speedway in Columbus, Ind., had more than racing on his mind before qualifying, and it wasn't the heat.

"As much as I love being home, I hate this week," he said. "I'll bet my phone rang 400 times last night because everybody knew that it was my only night off and everybody wanted to take me to dinner or go out and ride Harleys or do something.

"Between them and family and being home and wanting to do well in front of all your friends and family, that puts a lot of pressure on me."

Still, that didn't make winning his second pole of the season and sixth of his career any more gratifying for Stewart, who is determined to win this event.

"To be honest, I could care less about poles," he said. "I want my name on a brick and I want my name on a Borg-Warner trophy."

The winner of Indy's NASCAR race gets his name inscribed on one of the bricks that originally covered

> "To be honest, I could care less about poles. I want my name on a brick and I want my name on a Borg-Warner trophy."

the 2.5-mile Indy oval. The Borg-Warner trophy honors the winners of the Indianapolis 500.

Stewart was a star in the Indy Racing League before switching to stock cars. He raced in the Indianapolis 500 five times with a best finish of fifth in 1997 and is the only driver to start from the pole in the 500 and the Brickyard.

His best finish also is fifth in three previous stock car starts at Indy.

"I know the track," Stewart said. "If you look at the amount of laps that these Cup guys have, they probably

have as many laps or more than I've had here in the past. But being able to come here every day in the month of May for three or four weeks at a time, you learn some things day to day about the personality of the track and some things to watch out for."

The Dodge of Bill Elliott, coming off a victory from the pole a week ago at Pocono, took the outside spot on the front row at 182.109 mph, followed by the Chevrolet of Dale Earnhardt Jr. at 181.627, the Chevy of Robby Gordon at 181.543, and rookie Ryan Newman's Ford at 181.287.

Stewart noted that drawing the 11th spot in the qualifying line on the hot, humid day was a key to winning the pole.

"I think I lost about five pounds just in a few laps in a qualifying run," the stocky Stewart said. "I was never very good at drawing an early number. We've got somebody else doing it now, and he certainly earned his keep this week."

The temperature rose steadily and the humidity thickened as the session started at 11:05 a.m. and didn't end until 1:30 p.m.

The top four also were among the first 11 drivers in the line. Newman was the only driver to break the pattern, going out 49th among the 50 drivers who made attempts.

"It was in the heat of the day, but I think it was pretty hot from the time the first green flag dropped all the way through," Newman said. "It probably made a little bit of difference but, overall, the run was pretty good."

Newman, from South Bend, Ind. and a graduate of Purdue University, is 12th in the Winston Cup points but has yet to win a race. If he or teammate Rusty Wallace wins today, it would give team owner Roger Penske—who owns a record 11 Indianapolis 500 wins— his first stock car victory at the speedway. Wallace will start 35th in the 43-car field.

Three-time Brickyard winner Jeff Gordon won from 26th position last year and will start 21st, while two-time winner Dale Jarrett will start 17th.

Gordon, hoping to end a 28-race winless streak, said he was fortunate to qualify that high.

"Something just snapped in the motor when I crossed the line to complete the first lap," he said. "It could have happened during the lap. It just shut completely off. I'm hoping it's something in the driveline, not the motor."

If it does turn out to be the motor, under NASCAR's new rule permitting teams to use only one engine per race, his team could put a new engine in his Chevy. But Gordon, another local favorite who spent his teen years in nearby Pittsboro, Ind., would have to start from the rear of the field.

Ricky Rudd and Bobby Labonte, the only other former Brickyard winners in the lineup, also had problems in qualifying. Rudd, Jarrett's teammate, was 25th despite drawing the seventh spot in line. Labonte, going out in the middle of the session, had to use a provisional to take the 40th spot after failing to qualify by speed.

Kurt Busch, the fastest in practice Friday, also had to use a provisional after spinning in his first qualifying lap. He missed the wall but ruined his tires and will have to start 38th.

"The level of competition every week
is what keeps the flame going; if you enjoy a
challenge, Winston Cup racing will
give you one."

—Tony Stewart

DRIVER STEWART WINS AT WATKINS GLEN

By DICK BRINSTER, AP Sports Writer

August 11, 2002

WATKINS GLEN, N.Y. (AP) — As he begins his emotional healing process, Tony Stewart might do well to remember the words of old rival Robby Gordon.

"A little love," Gordon said when asked to describe his latest scrape with Stewart.

No, Stewart didn't get into another off-track altercation. On the 13th lap of the race Sunday, he hit Gordon, then held him off at the end to win at Watkins Glen International.

Stewart was racing for the first time since being placed

on a season-long probation for the second year in a row and fined $60,000 for punching a photographer Aug. 4 at the Brickyard 400 in Indianapolis. He's seeking professional help for his explosive temper but doesn't think the victory will begin to cure his problem.

"It's a Band-Aid," he said. "It's not going to heal me a bit."

But the tenor of Gordon—with whom Stewart once traded shoves in the garage area at Daytona—was one of respect for another aggressive racer without animosity born of defeat. Stewart also could learn from it.

"Tony tried to dive-bomb me," Gordon said of the move Stewart made at the end of the front straight on the 2.45-mile road course. "He locked up his brakes, got into the side of me. That's racing."

Although he had to spend most of his time after the race explaining how ashamed he was of himself for his

behavior a week earlier, Stewart might have unknowingly taken the first step on his road to recovery by easily accepting responsibility for hitting Gordon.

"It was my fault," Stewart said. "He gave me plenty of racing room down there on the bottom. I blew the corner and that's where the contact was."

Then, perhaps, came the second step in the self-healing process.

"I just kind of lifted to let him get his spot back because I wasn't going to take it by shoving him up the racetrack," Stewart said.

His Pontiac won by 1.636 seconds. It was his 15th career victory and third this year, matching Matt Kenseth for the most on the Winston Cup circuit.

Stewart hounded rookie Ryan Newman, who took the lead in his Ford on the 63rd of 90 laps, trying him inside and outside on the serpentine course. On the 72nd lap, the 31-year-old Stewart made his move on the 10th turn and completed it on the 11th and final corner on the 72nd lap.

"Tony got me there coming into 10, and I was driving with the mirror the rest of the way," Newman said.

Stewart got away from Gordon with a quick restart one-third of the way through the $3.6 million event and did the same thing to Newman when the green flag waved following caution periods that ended on the 76th and 82nd laps.

He survived one more restart after Kenny Wallace crashed hard into the foam wall on the 87th lap to bring out a race-halting red flag while the barrier was repaired. The race went green for a final lap—after a delay of 12 minutes, 45 seconds—but Stewart got the jump and drove away.

"I thought we still had a shot at it, but I wasn't ready for Tony to take off in Turn 10," Gordon said of the final restart. "He snookered us there."

But Stewart rejected the notion that he was jumping the restarts.

"They were laying back trying to get a run at me," he said. "As a driver I did my job, and that's to take away their advantage."

"They can say what they want, but we won it honest."

Newman, making his first start on a road course, finished a career-best second in his first start on a road course and got his fifth straight top five finish. Gordon was right behind him in his Chevrolet.

"I just kind of lifted to let him get his spot back because I wasn't going to take it by shoving him up the racetrack."

—Tony Stewart

P. J. Jones, in his first start for A. J. Foyt, finished fourth in a Pontiac. Pole-sitter Ricky Rudd, hoping to tie Jeff Gordon's record with a seventh road course victory, was fifth in a Pontiac.

The win moved Stewart from seventh to fourth in the standings, just 104 points behind series leader Sterling Marlin. Beset by an engine problem, Marlin finished 30th. He leads 10th-place finisher Mark Martin by 53 points in the overall standings.

Defending race champion Jeff Gordon, seeking to win for the fifth time in six years on the track, wound up 22nd.

"It's definitely disappointing because this is a place we run real well at," the four-time series champion said after his 30th straight defeat.

TONY STEWART

TONY STEWART

STEWART GETS CHAMPIONSHIP; COLLECTS MORE THAN $9 MILLION
By MIKE HARRIS, AP Motorsports Writer

HOMESTEAD, Florida (AP)—Unrelenting and unrepentant, Tony Stewart is NASCAR's new champion.

Racing's bad boy, the only driver ever to win a championship while on probation, didn't earn the title the way he would have liked. He finished 18th Sunday in the Ford 400 at Homestead-Miami Speedway.

That was enough, though, to keep runner-up Mark Martin at bay and win the championship by 38 points.

Kurt Busch, Martin's Roush Racing teammate, came on late to win the race, but his third victory in the last five events was almost completely overshadowed by the championship battle.

The often caustic and combative Stewart was uncharacteristically emotional, dabbing at his eyes and mopping his face with a towel before finally climbing from his No. 20 Pontiac.

"We really weren't that good today," Stewart said. "We got a lap down and that was pretty discouraging. I was awful nervous when we lost that lap, so it took a little bit of the pressure off when we got back on the lead lap.

"We never gave up. We never got frustrated with each other on the radio. We did this the way we got here, and that was as a team."

Stewart needed only to finish 22nd or better Sunday to clinch the title. Martin made a contest of it, finishing fourth and forcing Stewart to race hard for all 267 laps on the 1 1/2-mile oval. It just wasn't enough.

"Those guys were just a little bit stronger than us, but what an effort," said Martin, 43, now a four-time series runner-up and never a champion. "The only regret I have is that I could have provided more leadership to this team so we could have scored an extra 100 or 150 this year somewhere along the line, but we didn't and I couldn't."

Martin was docked 25 points after NASCAR discovered an unapproved spring on his Roush Racing Ford on Nov. 3 in Rockingham, N.C., or the final difference would have been even closer. An appeal of the penalty was turned down Saturday.

"We made it close," Martin said. "We gained points on the guy three races in a row so, in a way, I wish it wasn't over. I'm as proud of that as anything we did all year long."

"I still have a hard time believing we've done and accomplished what we've accomplished this year," Stewart said. "We didn't do anything magical. We didn't do anything special, but it was more of a personal victory for our team."

He gave much of the credit for the success to crew chief Greg Zipadelli.

"I practically destroyed this team by midseason, single-handedly, and Zippy was the glue that held everybody together," Stewart said. "Zippy was the friend that got me back on track and got my mindset right to do what we did the rest of the year."

Zipadelli shrugged off the compliment, saying, "We had a tough year; it's been up and down. It was worth it."

Joe Gibbs, who coached the Washington Redskins to three Super Bowl victories, now has two Winston Cup titles. Bobby Labonte, Stewart's teammate, won in 2000.

Stewart, who had won two of three previous races here, started sixth but never contended Sunday, driving a conservative race that saw him fall a lap behind the leaders on lap 192.

He hung in and got the lap back, moving onto the tail of the lead lap by passing then-leader Dale Jarrett on lap 205. He was able to stay ahead of the lead pack and, with the help of a yellow flag on lap 227, remained on the lead lap to the end.

"We've always run so good here. That's why it was such a surprise when the car went off like it did," Stewart said. "Luckily, Zippy did some aggressive changes to fix the thing. We got in the front of the pack again and were able to race the guys in the lead lap ahead of us.

"It wasn't a piece of cake by any means."

Stewart, NASCAR's Rookie of the Year in 1999, has won championships before—the last in 1997 in the Indy Racing League.

He finished fourth in the points as a rookie, sixth the next year, and a distant second to Gordon a year ago. Considered a favorite this season, Stewart got off to a disastrous start, blowing an engine and finishing last in the Daytona 500.

Asked to rate this title, he said, "They're all hard in their own way. But, to start the season off this year the way we did, 43rd in points after Daytona, to be able to rebound from all that, go through all the things that we went through this year and still keep our focus, to get the points that we needed to do what we did this year, it's incredible."

It took until the second half of the season for Stewart to get hot. As other leaders stumbled in front of him, he moved to the top on Oct. 6 in Talladega, the 30th race of the 36-race season, and stayed there.

Stewart grew up racing on the Midwest's short tracks, on dirt and pavement. In 1995, he became the first driver to win the U.S. Auto Club's midget, sprint and Silver Crown series in the same season.

He acknowledges his first love is racing at the smaller tracks where he doesn't have to deal with hordes of fans and media.

Martin said Stewart, off-track troubles or no, is a deserving champion.

"Down deep, I'm just like Tony," Martin said. "I'd rather be down the road at a dirt track. He's a racer's racer and he's really, really good."

Tony Stewart's differences with the media and NASCAR officials are well chronicled, and he made light of them Friday night in New York while being honored as the Winston Cup champion.

Last year, after being forced by NASCAR to obey a new rule and wear a head and neck restraint device, Stewart pretended to be hot on the podium as he accepted his second-place check. He mopped his brow, took off the jacket of his Tuxedo and exposed a head and neck restraint.

This time he topped himself and got plenty of laughs from those who remembered he finished a second straight season on probation after punching a photographer. Stewart pulled a camera from under the podium and began shooting pictures of the cameramen who were photographing him.

"I've just been a regular media darling this week," he said.

And it didn't end there. Making light of his anger management sessions. Stewart poked fun at NASCAR president Mike Helton and pulled out a piece of paper wrapped in a red ribbon.

"Mike said I had to show him I had my anger management certificate to prove I finished the course," he said. "This is it."

Then he turned serious for a moment and addressed the media, some of whom he has refused to deal with in the past.

"I know you've got a job to do," Stewart said. "I promise to do a better job dealing with you guys next year."

Earlier, Stewart said he wasn't in racing for the money. Still, he wasn't about to give back the more than $9 million he received at the awards ceremony.

"This is all great, but I don't care if I win a lot of money at a Winston Cup race or win nothing running a sprint car at some little track. I just want to race," Stewart said.

The 31-year-old Stewart definitely wasn't in his element Friday night as he was handed checks totaling $9,163,761.

That includes $4,305,607 from the season points fund, as well as season earnings and postseason bonus and contingency money. The total raises Stewart's career earnings to just over $20.9 million in four seasons.

"That's just awesome," said Stewart, who has had a whirlwind week of celebration, starting on Monday with a visit with President Bush at the White House.

Stewart, who admittedly dislikes interviews, public speaking and signing autographs, has been the picture of cooperation since embarking on what NASCAR calls "Champion's Week."

The hot-tempered driver who has repeatedly gotten into trouble with NASCAR, has smiled a lot this week, happily signing autographs for anyone who approached him and giving interviews readily.

"I've even enjoyed talking with the media," he said, laughing. "I don't think anybody thought they'd ever hear that out of me. But it's all been very relaxing and a lot of fun."

All this doesn't necessarily signal any change in Stewart's ways in 2003.

Late in the 2002 season, as Stewart battled Mark Martin for the title he eventually won by just 38 points, Stewart said that winning a championship would not make him a spokesman for the sport.

On Friday, even as he prepared to accept all the accolades that go with the title, that opinion had not changed.

"To be honest, I still don't feel like I'm a representative or an ambassador for the sport," he said. "I'm just a simple boy from Indiana. I don't want to be a legend or an icon or anything. I just want to be a race car driver, pure and simple.

"But, going through this last week, it's given me more of an appreciation for what's happened this year. It's easier to put it all in perspective."

Stewart is already looking forward to getting into uniform for preseason testing.

"You know, by January, this will all be done," he said. "I'm going to put on a new pair of gloves, a new pair of racing shoes and my helmet and go out and race for another championship.

"What I did this season won't make any difference any more."

During the ceremony, Stewart paid tribute to car owner Joe Gibbs, crew chief Greg Zipadelli, engine builder Mark Cronquist and the rest of his team.

"Every person on this team, from Joe on down, contributed to this championship," Stewart said. "I just drove the car."

"We knew he would win a championship and I'm glad this team could help him do it," Gibbs said. "I believe Tony is going to win more of them, too."

Zipadelli, also winning his first championship, got a bonus from his driver earlier in the day.

"I promised Zippy if we won the championship, I'd buy him a Corvette," Stewart said.

On Friday morning, Stewart presented the keys to a red Corvette to Zipadelli outside a midtown hotel.

"That's the kind of stuff that makes this fun," Stewart said.

Photo Credits

AP/Wide World Photos:

Caroline Baird—85

Jamie Belk—126, 129

Gerry Broome—5

Rusty Burroughs—73

Chuck Burton—66, 89, 161

J. Pat Carter—159

Stephen Chernin—162, 165

Amy E. Conn—16, 19

Paul Connors—103

Michael Conroy—86

Peter Cosgrove—23

Pat Crowe II—97

Darron Cummings—130, 131, 142, 143, 145, 146

Alan Diaz—37

David Duprey—148, 149, 150, 153, 155

Ric Feld—100, 114, 115

Mike Fiala—12, 14

Kevin Glackmeyer—90, 95

David Graham—108, 113

Tony Gutierrez—42, 46

Russ Hamilton—62, 71, 151, 154

John Harrell—3

Steve Helber —
    1, 7, 9, 32, 33, 65, 80, 118, 119, 122, 123

Dean Hoffmeyer—6

Julie Jacobson—135,141

Bob Jordan—104

Dave Kennedy—75, 134, 136, 137, 140

Paul Kizzle—111

Jay LaPrete—70

Wilfredo Lee—109

Sandy Macys—38

Phil Manson—101

Ben Margot—22, 55

Dave Martin—39, 99

Chuck McQuinn—60, 61

Pablo Martinez Monsivais—163

Kevin Morley—121, 124, 125

George Nikitin—76, 77

Chris O'Meara—10, 11, 25, 44, 45, 51, 59, 83

Carl Pendleton—92

Terry Renna—43, 110, 112, 133

Kevin Rivoli—156, 157

Paul Sancya—158

Joe Sebo—49

Glenn Smith—105

Tom Strattman—79

Jim Topper—56

Nick Wass—21, 26, 27, 28, 29, 31

Craig Williby—36, 41

Getty Images:

Darrell Ingham—52

Robert Laberge—67, 69

Jamie Squire—94, 117

Audio Credits

MARK GARROW: With a Dad who was a flagman and a mom who scored races at their local short track, Mark Garrow has been around racing just about his whole life. He's spent the last two decades as a radio and television broadcaster following NASCAR's top circuit.

Currently, Mark serves as co-anchor for the race broadcasts on The Performance Racing Network (PRN). He also hosts PRN's Garage Pass, a daily show heard on over 450 radio stations nationwide and NASCAR.com, providing fans with the latest NASCAR news. Considered one of the hardest-working journalists in motorsports today, Mark has earned numerous awards for his work. He resides in Lexington, N.C., with his wife, Lynne, and their children, Breanna and Marissa.